What the Standards say about ...

FOSTERING

Meral Mehmet

Russell House Publishing

First published in 2005 by:
Russell House Publishing Ltd.
4 St. George's House
Uplyme Road
Lyme Regis
Dorset DT7 3LS

Tel: 01297-443948
Fax: 01297-442722
e-mail: help@russellhouse.co.uk
www.russellhouse.co.uk

© Meral Mehmet

The moral right of Meral Mehmet to be identified as the author of this work has been asserted by her in accordance with The Copyright Designs and Patents Act (1988).

All rights reserved. No part of this publication may be reproduced, stored in a retrieval system or transmitted in any form, or by any means, electronic, mechanical, photocopying, recording or otherwise, without the prior permission of the copyright holder and the publisher.

British Library Cataloguing-in-publication Data:
A catalogue record for this book is available from the British Library.

ISBN: 1-903855-47-0

Design and layout by Jeremy Spencer
Printed by Antony Rowe, Chippenham

About Russell House Publishing

RHP is a group of social work, probation, education and youth and community work practitioners and academics working in collaboration with a professional publishing team. Our aim is to work closely with the field to produce innovative and valuable materials to help managers, trainers, practitioners and students.
We are keen to receive feedback on publications and new ideas for future projects.
For details of our other publications please visit our website or ask us for a catalogue.
Contact details are on this page.

Contents

Foreword	vii
Acknowledgements	viii
1. Introduction	1
2. Why are there Two Sets of Standards?	3
How do the two sets of standards work together?	4
What does this mean for you?	4
3. Summary of the *UK National Standards for Foster Care* (UKNS)	5
4. Summary of the *National Minimum Standards for Fostering Services* (NMS)	8
5. Recruiting Carers	11
What does this mean for you?	12
What should you consider when applying to foster	12
Carers task description: overall summary	13
The competencies needed for foster care	14
6. Assessing Carers	16
The assessment of foster carers	16
What does this mean for you?	17
The checks undertaken on all carers, their household and support networks	18
7. The Fostering Panel	20
The fostering panel	20
What does this mean for you?	22
8. The Foster Care Agreement	23
The Foster Care Agreement	23
What the regulations say	23
What does this mean for you?	24
What is the difference between being approved by the foster care panel and the Foster Care Agreement?	24
9. Terms and Conditions for Foster Carers	25
Terms and conditions for foster carers	25
10. Supervision and Support	27
Supervision/support/advice/information	27
What does this mean for you?	28
The role of the young person's social worker	29
The role of the supervising social worker	31
Support groups	32
Support carers/support network	32

11.	**Training**	**33**
	Training	33
	What does this mean for you?	34

12.	**Listening to and Involving Children**	**35**
	A child's right to be listened to	35

13.	**Valuing the Diversity of the Child**	**36**
	Valuing diversity	36
	What does this mean for you?	37

14.	**Children Being Placed With You**	**38**
	Matching children into your home	38
	What does this mean for you?	39
	What should I do when preparing for a placement?	40
	What authority do I have to look after children/young people?	41
	What if parents want to remove their child from my home?	41

15.	**Looked After Children Documents**	**42**
	Children's documents	42
	What does this mean for you?	46
	Supplementary documents kept on the child or young person	46
	The Assessment and Progress records	47

16.	**Keeping Records and Accessing Records**	**48**
	Record keeping	48
	What does this mean for you?	49
	Some guidance about recording	50
	How long should I keep my records for?	51
	Access to records	51

17.	**Confidentiality**	**52**
	Confidentiality	52
	What does this mean for you?	52
	A cover story	52

18.	**Safety in the Home**	**53**
	Health and safety in the foster home	53
	What does this mean for you?	53
	The child or young person's general health and welfare	56
	Managing some risks	56
	Reporting accidents or incidents	56
	Pets and animals	57

19.	**Safer Caring**	**58**
	Safer caring	58
	What does this mean for you?	59
	Other things to remember about safer caring	60

20.	**Child Protection**	**61**
	Child protection	61
	Your role when a child/young person tells you that they have been abused	61
	The principles of child protection	62
	Your role in the child protection process	63
	The child protection register	63
	What are the definitions of child abuse?	63
21.	**Children's Health**	**67**
	Health	67
	National Healthy Care Standards (NHCS)	68
	What does this mean for you?	69
	Dental care	70
	Eye care	71
	The wishes and feelings of children and consent	71
	Sexual health/sex education	71
	If the young person is sexually active and over 16 years of age	72
	Pregnancy	73
	Getting treatment for sexually transmitted diseases/infectious diseases	73
	Alcohol, drugs and solvent abuse	75
22.	**Contact**	**77**
	Contact	77
	What does this mean for you?	78
	Working with parents/parental responsibility	80
	Social work visits	81
23.	**Education**	**82**
	The education of children looked after	82
	What does this mean for you?	83
	The government's performance indicators for the education of looked after children	84
	Education plans	84
	What is my role as a carer?	85
	Statement of educational needs	86
	Leisure activities	86
24.	**Leaving Care/After Care**	**87**
	Leaving care/After care	87
	What does this mean for you?	88
	Connexions (England only)	89
	Transition into adult life	89
	How should we all be working to prepare young people?	89
	What should carers be doing to prepare young people?	90
	What is a pathway plan?	91
	Pathway planning	91
	Role of the personal advisors	92
25.	**Managing a Child's Behaviour**	**93**
	Managing behaviour	93
	Methods of control and discipline	93

What does this mean for you?	94
Encouraging positive behaviour	95
Understanding your own reactions and responses	95

26. When a Child is Missing From Home — 96
When a child/young person is missing from home — 96
Before reporting a child as missing — 97
How to respond when the young person returns — 97

27. Bullying — 99
What is bullying? — 99
Why do some children bully? — 99
Signs that a child may be bullied — 100
Some of the long-term consequences of being bullied — 100
Guidance on tackling bullying — 100
How to work with the school — 100

28. Children Making Complaints — 101
Making a complaint — 101
What does this mean for you? — 102
Complaints policy and procedure — 102
Why do children and young people make complaints and allegations against carers? — 103

29. Carers Making Complaints and Allegations Made Against Carers — 104
Complaints and allegations — 104
What does this mean for you? — 105
Allegations or complaints against carers — 105

30. Annual Reviews — 107
Annual reviews — 107
What does this mean for you? — 108
Why are annual reviews carried out? — 108
Who should contribute to an annual review? — 109
What other things will be included in the annual review? — 110

31. Termination of Approval — 111
Termination of approval/agreement — 111
What does termination of approval mean? — 111
What do I have to do if I want to leave my fostering agency or local authority? — 112
The Fostering Network/Independent Agencies Protocol — 113

32. Whistle-Blowing — 114
Whistle-blowing — 114

Appendix 1   The Foster Placement Agreement — 115
Appendix 2   The Foster Care Register — 116
Appendix 3   The Statement of Purpose — 117
Appendix 4   Useful contact details for children looked after — 118

Bibliography — 119

Foreword

As an adult who once spent five lovely years in foster care, reading these guidelines enabled me to look back on my own experience and evaluate.

It is imperative that good structured guidelines are introduced to foster carers, social workers and anyone else who plays a role in the lives of looked after children and young people.

My own experience was extremely positive, I always felt supported, empowered and listened to. I hope the guidelines will enable all children and young people to have the same experience.

I have written about being looked after and am an independent panel member sitting on four panels. I also do freelance social care work and will be encouraging all the professionals I meet to read these guidelines so that they can help looked after children and young people have the very best start in life.

Sheryl Penrose

Acknowledgements

The top of my list for thanks must go to the two central women involved in encouraging me with this guide. Both Ena Fry and Ann Wheal graced me with their presence one June evening last year and by the time they had left, I had more or less agreed to write this guide. I thank you both wholeheartedly.

Other thanks are to: Parents for Children, First Choice Foster Care, ProTeen and East London Foster Care – all who kindly commissioned me to do work for them that paved the way for the guide.

Other special people who helped me shape the guide include Meti Taddesse, Sheryl Penrose and Sheryl's foster mum, who read the guide and offered invaluable critique.

And Geoffrey.

Last but not least, my partner Kemal – just for being around.

Chapter 1

Introduction

The publication of two sets of standards – the *UK National Standards for Foster Care* and the *Code of Practice* ('best practice') and the *National Minimum Standards for Fostering Services* with its accompanying *Fostering Services Regulations (2002)* – has set a new framework for foster care.

What the Standards Say about ... Fostering examines the two sets of standards, looks beyond what is literally being said and interprets them for practical everyday use.

In this book, the treatment of certain aspects of fostering has been deliberate:

- There is no specific chapter on children with disabilities, since all children should be treated and cared for in the best possible way.
- The chapter on *Listening to and Involving Children* has been kept quite short. Since listening to and involving children is such an intrinsic part of fostering (and an absolute right) it would not make sense to limit the reader to what is contained in a single chapter as the whole guide is dedicated to working effectively with children.
- The subject of 'family and friends as carers' has been integrated into the guide, rather than being dealt with separately, because this group should be treated no differently from 'ordinary' foster carers in terms of support, care and guidance.

The chapters follow the process of *becoming* a foster carer and then go on to deal with aspects of being a foster carer. However, to enable you to dip into it at any time, the chapters are self contained and have references to other chapters and sources of further information.

How this guide will help you

Using this guide will help you to:

- Identify what the standards say and where to find them.
- Ensure children and young people are involved in everything that affects their lives.
- Identify the range of responsibilities in foster care.
- Identify what your rights are as a foster carer and what you can expect from the fostering agency.
- Show how different professionals should work together.
- Consider best child care practice.
- Help children to identify their rights in foster care.
- Identify useful checklists.
- *Help you to look at how you and your household foster prior to being inspected.

Who this guide is for

Whilst written from the perspective of foster carers, this guide is an essential reference material for them and for all professionals who work in fostering including:

- *Supervising social workers in local authorities – as a supervision and inspection tool with foster carers.
- *Supervising social workers in fostering agencies – as a supervision and inspection tool with foster carers.
- Children and family social workers – to ensure that the standards for the child in foster care are being upheld.
- Social services fostering managers – as a reminder and a tool for looking at best practice and beyond. Also to ensure that statutory requirements are being met.
- *Inspectors of fostering services – to ensure that the standards are being clearly evidenced.
- Members of fostering panels – as a reference guide to ensure good, consistent assessments of foster carers and good consistent standards in the annual review process.
- Complaints officers – as a reference point when dealing with complaints from carers or children who have been fostered.
- Local authority councillors – who have responsibilities placed upon them to ensure children who are fostered receive the best possible service and support.
- Voluntary and national fostering agencies.
- Children's rights agencies.
- And finally a useful guide for children who are or have been fostered.

*All those involved in providing services for children and young people in foster care will be inspected regularly. While the primary tools used to inspect will be the *National Minimum Standards for Fostering Services*, inspectors will also expect the *UK National Standards for Foster Care* and the *Code of Practice* to be 'fully complied' with (see Chapter 2).

How to use the guide

The guide is divided into chapters that cover the activities and responsibilities of the foster carer and the fostering service. Most chapters start with the relevant *National Minimum Standards for Fostering Services* (NMS) and then expand on this where necessary by referring to the *UK National Standards for Foster Care* (UKNS). Most chapters then have a section called *What does this mean for you?* which explains the standards from a foster carer's perspective and give either examples of good practice or more information to help expand the meaning of the standards.

Chapter 3

Summary of the UK National Standards for Foster Care *(UKNS)*

This summary of the *UK National Standards for Foster Care* is published by permission of the Fostering Network.

Section 1: The specific needs and rights of each child or young person in foster care are met and respected (Standards 1-12)

Standard 1   **Equal opportunities and valuing diversity:** Children and young people, and their families, are provided with foster care services which value diversity and promote equality.

Standard 2   **Assessment of the child's or young person's needs:** An assessment of the child's or young person's needs is made prior to any placement, communicated to all parties concerned and updated regularly.

Standard 3   **Care planning and reviews:** A written care plan is prepared for each child or young person placed in foster care; all aspects of the plan are implemented, it is reviewed regularly and any changes are made only as a result of a review meeting.

Standard 4   **Matching carers with children or young people:** Each child or young person placed in foster care is carefully matched with a carer capable of meeting her or his assessed needs.

Standard 5   **The child's or young person's social worker:** Each child or young person placed in foster care has a designated social worker who ensures statutory requirements for her or his care and protection are met and promotes her or his welfare and development.

Standard 6   **A safe and positive environment:** The foster home provides a safe, healthy and nurturing environment for the child or young person.

Standard 7   **Safe caring:** Each child or young person in foster care is protected from all forms of abuse, neglect, exploitation and deprivation.

Standard 8   **Recording and access to information:** An up-to-date comprehensive case record is maintained for each child or young person in foster care which details the nature and quality of care provided and contributes to an understanding of her or his life events; relevant information from the case record is made available to the child and to anyone involved in her or his care.

Standard 9 **Contact between children and their families and friends:** Each child or young person in foster care is encouraged to maintain and develop family contacts and friendships as set out in her or his care plan and/or placement agreement.

Standard 10 **Health care and development:** Each child or young person in foster care receives health care which meets her or his needs for physical, emotional and social growth, together with information and training appropriate to her or his age and understanding to enable informed participation in decisions about her or his health needs.

Standard 11 **Educational needs:** The learning and educational needs of each child or young person in foster care are given high priority and she or he is encouraged to attain her or his full potential.

Standard 12 **Preparation for adult life:** Each child or young person in foster care is helped to develop the skills, competence and knowledge necessary for adult living; she or he receives appropriate support and guidance for as long as necessary after being in foster care.

Section 2: Effective and appropriate care is provided by each foster carer (Standards 13-17)

Standard 13 **Assessment and approval of foster carers:** Each foster carer is subject to and participates in a comprehensive assessment of her or his ability to carry out the fostering task and must be formally approved by the appropriate authority before a child or young person is placed in her or his care.

Standard 14 **Supervision, support, information and advice for foster carers:** Each approved foster carer is supervised by a named, appropriately qualified social worker and has access to adequate social work and other professional support, information and advice to enable her or him to provide consistent, high quality care for each child or young person placed in her or his home.

Standard 15 **Training of foster carers:** Each foster carer is provided with the training necessary to equip her or him with the skills and knowledge to provide high quality care for each child or young person placed in her or his care.

Standard 16 **Annual reviews with carers:** A joint review is conducted with each carer at least once a year in a manner that satisfies the authority of the continuing capacity of the carer to carry out the fostering task, provides the carer with an opportunity to give feedback, contributes to essential information on the quality and range of service provided by the authority, and informs recruitment, assessment and training strategies.

Standard 17 **Payment of allowances and expenses associated with caring for fostered children:** Each foster carer receives an allowance and agreed expenses which cover the full cost of caring for each child or young person placed with her or him.

Section 3: Each authority responsible for the provision of public care for children and young people offers a high quality foster care service for all who could benefit from it (Standards 18-25)

Standard 18   **Effective policies:** Each authority has effective policies in place to promote and plan the provision of high quality foster care for children and young people who could benefit from it.

Standard 19   **Management structures:** Each authority has effective structures in place for the management and supervision of foster care services, staff and foster carers.

Standard 20   **Professional qualifications and appropriate training for social workers:** All social work staff responsible for the provision of fostering services are professionally qualified and appropriately trained to work with children and young people, their families and foster carers, and have a good understanding of foster care.

Standard 21   **Recruiting and retaining an appropriate range of carers:** Each authority ensures access to a supply of foster carers which meets the range of needs of the children and young people within its area.

Standard 22   **Reward payments to carers:** Each authority considers the implementation of a reward payment scheme for foster carers.

Standard 23   **The foster care panel:** Each authority convenes a fostering panel as part of its assessment and approval process for foster carers, which also plays a role in monitoring and developing local fostering policy, procedures and practice.

Standard 24   **Placement of children through other authorities or agencies:** Where an authority contracts out any aspect of the provision of foster care for a child or young person it is looking after with another authority or agency, the authority responsible for the care of the child ensures that legal requirements for her or his care are met and the care provided meets national quality standards and regulations for the foster care service.

Standard 25   **Representations and complaints procedures:** Children and young people, their parents, foster carers and other people involved are able to make effective representations, including complaints, about any aspect of the fostering service, whether it is provided directly by an authority or by a contracted authority or agency.

Chapter 4

Summary of the National Minimum Standards for Fostering Services (NMS)

These standards have been reproduced, with permission, from the DoH's *National Minimum Standards for Fostering Services* and the accompanying *Fostering Services Regulations 2002*.

Statement of purpose (Standards 1-3)

Standard 1 There is a clear statement of the aims and objectives of the fostering service and of what facilities and services they provide.

Standard 2 The people involved in carrying on and managing the fostering service possess the necessary business and management skills and financial expertise to manage the work efficiently and effectively and have the necessary knowledge and experience of child care and fostering to do so in a professional manner.

Standard 3 Any persons carrying on or managing the fostering service are suitable people to run a business concerned with safeguarding and promoting the welfare of children.

Management of the fostering service (Standards 4-5)

Standard 4 There are clear procedures for monitoring and controlling the activities of the fostering service and ensuring quality performance.

Standard 5 The fostering service is managed effectively and efficiently.

Securing and promoting welfare (Standards 6-14)

Standard 6 The fostering service makes available foster carers who provide a safe, healthy and nurturing environment.

Standard 7 The fostering service ensures that children and young people, and their families, are provided with foster care services which value diversity and promote equality.

Standard 8 Local authority fostering services, and voluntary agencies placing children in their own right, ensure that each child or young person placed in foster care is carefully matched with a carer capable of meeting her/his assessed needs. For agencies providing foster carers to local authorities, those agencies ensure that they offer carers only if they represent appropriate matches for a child for whom a local authority is seeking a carer.

Standard 9   The fostering service protects each child or young person from all forms of abuse, neglect, exploitation and deprivation.

Standard 10 The fostering service makes sure that each child or young person in foster care is encouraged to maintain and develop family contacts and friendships as set out in her/his care plan and/or foster placement agreement.

Standard 11 The fostering service ensures that children's opinions, and those of their families and others significant to the child, are sought over all issues which are likely to affect their daily life and their future.

Standard 12 The fostering service ensures that it provides foster care services which help each child or young person in foster care to receive health care which meets her/his needs for physical, emotional and social development, together with information and training appropriate to her/his age and understanding to enable informed participation in decisions about her/his health needs.

Standard 13 The fostering service gives a high priority to meeting the educational needs of each child or young person in foster care and ensures that she/he is encouraged to attain her/his full potential.

Standard 14 The fostering service ensures that their foster care services help to develop skills, competence and knowledge necessary for adult living.

Recruiting, checking, managing, supporting and training staff and foster carers (Standards 15-23)

Standard 15 Any people working in or for the fostering service are suitable people to work with children and young people and to safeguard and promote their welfare.

Standard 16 Staff are organised and managed in a way which delivers an efficient and effective foster care service.

Standard 17 The fostering service has an adequate number of sufficiently experienced and qualified staff and recruits a range of carers to meet the needs of children and young people for whom it aims to provide a service.

Standard 18 The fostering service is a fair and competent employer, with sound employment practices and good support for its staff and carers.

Standard 19 There is a good quality training programme to enhance individual skills and to keep staff up-to-date with professional and legal developments.

Standard 20 All staff are properly accountable and supported.

Standard 21 The fostering service has a clear strategy for working with and supporting carers.

Standard 22 The fostering service is a managed one which provides supervision for foster carers and helps them to develop their skills.

Standard 23 The fostering service ensures that foster carers are trained in the skills required to provide high quality care and meet the needs of each child/young person placed in their care.

Records (Standards 24-25)

Standard 24 The fostering service ensures that an up-to-date, comprehensive case record is maintained for each child or young person in foster care which details the nature and quality of care provided and contributes to an understanding of her/his life events. Relevant information from the case records is made available to the child and to anyone involved in her/his care.

Standard 25 The fostering service's administrative records contain all significant information relevant to the running of the foster care service and as required by regulations.

Fitness of premises for use as a fostering service (Standards 26-32)

Standard 26 Premises used as offices by the fostering service are appropriate for the purpose.

Standard 27 The agency ensures it is financially viable at all times and has sufficient financial resources to fulfil its obligations.

Standard 28 The financial processes/systems of the agency are properly operated and maintained in accordance with sound and appropriate accounting standards and practice.

Standard 29 Each foster carer receives an allowance and agreed expenses, which cover the full cost of caring for each child or young person placed with him or her. Payments are made promptly and at the agreed time. Allowances and fees are reviewed annually.

Standard 30 Fostering panels have clear written policies and procedures, which are implemented in practice, about the handling of their functions.

Standard 31 Where a fostering service provides short-term breaks for children in foster care, they have policies and procedures, implemented in practice, to meet the particular needs of children receiving short-term breaks.

Standard 32 These standards are all relevant to carers who are family and friends of the child, but there is a recognition of the particular relationship and position of family and friends carers.

Chapter 5

Recruiting Carers

The fostering service have a recruitment policy and strategies aimed at ensuring they recruit the range of carers to meet the needs of all the children they provide a service for.
NMS 17.5

NMS The National Minimum Standards also say the *fostering service* must ensure that:

- These strategies include how they will ensure the type of people recruited will be safe carers (and workers) and will promote and safeguard all children in their care (**NMS 15.1**).
- They have enough qualified staff to recruit the range of carers they need (**NMS 17.1**) and their administrative procedures work well and are effective (**NMS 16.10**), and ensure enquiries from prospective carers are dealt with promptly (**NMS 16.12**).

- Where an application is made from a member of a child's family or someone closely connected to them, that it is recognised that they could provide a potentially good placement for the child (**NMS 32.1, NMS 32.2**), that they are supported and trained in the way all carers should be (**NMS 32.3**) and that the way the fostering agency works with them makes it easy for them to put themselves forward as carers for the child (**NMS 32.4**).

UKNS The UK National Standards for Foster Care include the following:

- That the recruitment strategy recognises the knowledge and experience of existing carers and children who have been fostered; and that the fostering service fully encourages their contributions to the planning and implementation of recruiting new carers (**UKNS 21.6**).
- That all recruitment strategies are reviewed annually and modified, using all available research and information specifically on the terms and conditions provided to carers is used to ensure they are as effective as they can be (**UKNS 21.9 and 21.12**).
- All potential foster carers are provided with a comprehensive range of information on the task of fostering which includes a job or task profile and job or task specification for foster carers (**UKNS 21.7**).
- That every new enquiry is responded to within two weeks (**UKNS 21.8**).
- That polices, procedures and the standards of each fostering agency *understand* the importance of retaining their carers and clearly work towards this (**UKNS 21.10**).

What does this mean for you?

The standards emphasise the need for fostering agencies to have clearly thought out and written recruitment polices that look not only at recruiting carers but are also wide ranging. They place a large emphasis on the retention of their carers and in support of this are research findings that show that retention is a very effective way of recruiting carers. Carers who are satisfied with their agency and enjoy fostering will tell and encourage others to apply, while those who remain in fostering become more experienced.

The standards also place emphasis on the need for the agency to be well staffed and skilled and that all new enquiries made should be responded to within at least two weeks.

What should you consider when applying to foster?

Many people may apply to become a carer but few will successfully go through to the assessment and then the approval stage. This is because, while a wide diversity of people are welcomed and encouraged to foster, fostering is a highly skilled task and your agency's role is to be able to identify those who have the skill or the potential to fulfil these requirements. There are rigorous checks as well as a detailed assessment process to undergo. Training is also compulsory and for couple households, both adults need to complete the training.

The most obvious issues when considering your selection as a potential carer is that your agency needs to be satisfied that you have the *availability*, the *qualities*, the *competence* and the *aptitude* for caring. You may be highly skilled but if you do not have the time to care for a young person then you may not be able to undertake the full responsibilities of fostering. You must also be able to show evidence that you and your friends and family networks are trustworthy, do not have any convictions which would prevent you from being a carer and do not have any concerns over your work in the caring field.

There are of course, other more practical factors to be considered, some of which are as follows:

- You must have a space in your home, many agencies require a spare bedroom for the child you are asked to care for.
- Have space for young people to play or do homework.
- Be able to meet the needs of children you have living with you and to show that you have the ability to care for other children.
- Be able to attend meetings and have time during the day to do so.
- Must be able to show that you have a strong and supportive network who are able to help you where appropriate.

Your initial enquiry is crucial as it is the first contact with an agency and should be positive. You should be given good, clear information at this stage to enable you to decide if you wish to continue or not. In order to do this you will need:

- Information about what it means to foster.
- Information about children who are looked after.
- Information about the different types of fostering schemes.
- The agency job/task description and specification.
- A copy of the competencies for foster carers and other details about the assessment.
- Information about the terms and conditions of being a foster carer including details of payments and allowances.

We have reproduced below with kind permission from the Fostering Network their proposed job/task description and the fostering competencies for your information.

Carer's task description: overall summary

To be responsible for the care in one's own home of a child(ren) or young person placed by an authority, and to work with the agency and all those involved in helping children fulfil their potential.

Caring for children
1.1 To provide day-to-day care of the children being looked after, having regard to the particular demands on children separated from their families.
1.2 To take part in implementing the child care plan, which would include specific tasks and, often, contact with parents and others who are important to the child.
1.3 To promote the healthy growth and development of the child or children, with particular emphasis on health and on educational achievement.
1.4 To ensure that the children being looked after are encouraged in a positive understanding of their origins, religion and culture.
1.5 To assist and support parents and other people who are significant in a child's life to sustain and develop relations with them.
1.6 To enable children and young people who are moving on to do so in a positive manner.

Providing a safe and caring environment
2.1 To ensure that children are kept safe from harm or abuse and that they are taught how to get help should anything untoward occur.
2.2 To promote the secure attachment of children to adults capable of providing safe and effective care.
2.3 To act as an advocate for each child.

Working as part of a team
3.1 To be part of the agency and work with other agency staff and professionals within agency guidelines, policies and procedures.
3.2. To attend and actively participate in all reviews, family meetings, case conferences and court hearings as required, and to keep written records of placements and contribute to reports.
3.3. To take up appropriate training opportunities and recognise the benefit of continued training.
3.4. To deal responsibly with confidential information.

The competencies needed for foster care

Caring for children
1.1 An ability to provide a good standard of care to other people's children which promotes healthy emotional, physical and sexual development as well as their health and education.
1.2 An ability to work closely with children's families and others who are important to the child.
1.3 An ability to set appropriate boundaries, and manage children's behaviour within these, without the use of physical or other inappropriate punishment.
1.4 Knowledge of normal child development and an ability to listen to and communicate with children appropriate to their age and understanding.

Providing a safe and caring environment
2.1 An ability to ensure that children are cared for in a home where they are safe from harm or abuse.
2.2 An ability to help children keep safe from harm or abuse, and to know how to seek help if their safety is threatened.

Working as part of a team
3.1 An ability to work with other professional people and contribute to the departments planning for the child/young person.
3.2 An ability to communicate effectively.
3.3 An ability to keep information confidential.
3.4 An ability to promote equality, diversity and rights of individuals and groups within society.

Own development
4.1 An ability to appreciate how personal experiences have affected themselves and their families, and the impact fostering is likely to have on them all.
4.2 An ability to have people and links within the community which provide support.
4.3 An ability to use training opportunities and to improve skills.
4.4 An ability to sustain positive relationships and maintain effective functioning through periods of stress.

As indicated above, the initial stage is very much an information sharing process with the agency giving you details about themselves and fostering and them in turn seeking information to enable them to continue with your application. There are a number of elements to this initial stage:

- open day/information day
- a home visit
- preparation group

Open day/information day
Some agencies organise such events usually after a recruitment campaign. These events give people who are interested in fostering the opportunity to meet with agency staff, other carers, ask questions, and seek further information.

Home visit
The home visit is sometimes considered a 'mini' fostering assessment in itself and is a detailed piece of work which has to be written into a report. The information contained in the report will ultimately indicate whether your application is to go on to a full fostering assessment.

The person undertaking the home visit will look at your home to check its suitability for fostering. They may offer advice about how to make it more compatible for fostering but this will also be taken up later if an assessment is started.

Preparation group
These are training days organised by the agency to start to prepare potential carers for the task and role of fostering. They should provide you with the range of knowledge to enable you, once you have been assessed, to commence fostering. Where there are two adults in the house both will be expected to complete the preparation training.

For details of what should be contained in the preparation stage see Chapter 6 *Assessing Carers*.

It should still be made clear to you that you can decide not to continue at any stage of this process.

Chapter 6

Assessing Carers

The assessment of foster carers

There is a clearly set out assessment process for carers which defines:
- *the task to be undertaken*
- *the qualities, competences or aptitudes being sought or to be achieved*
- *the standards to be applied in the assessment*
- *the stages and content of the selection process and the timescales involved*
- *the information to be given to applicants*

NMS 17.6

NMS The National Minimum Standards also say the *fostering service* must ensure that:

- All staff who carry out assessments are suitably knowledgeable, qualified, trained and experienced in assessments and family placement work. Where a student is to undertake the assessment, a member of staff who has these requirements takes overall responsibility for the assessment and supervises the student (**NMS 15.5** and **NMS 15.6**).
- All potential carers are interviewed and references are taken up and these references should be checked (**NMS 15.3**).
- Records are kept of all references. Police checks are renewed every three years (**NMS 15.4**).
- The important role carers have in helping and supporting the child to maintain links with their parents and other people important to them, is especially stressed at this stage (**NMS 10.5**) so is the importance of safer caring (**NMS 23.6**).
- All potential carers are offered the opportunity to meet and benefit from the knowledge of existing carers. All newcomers must also be given induction training (**NMS 23.2**).
- Preparation groups are run at different places and times to enable everyone to attend and the agency should provide childcare or reasonable expenses to cover costs incurred for child care (**NMS 23.3**).
- All the training promotes equal opportunities and anti-discriminatory practice (**NMS 23.3**).
- Where there are two adults in the household, both adults must undertake all the preparation training and that the agency should address specific issues that are relevant to particular groups e.g. male carers, carers from diverse backgrounds, carers with disabilities (**NMS 23.4**) as well as sons and daughters of potential foster carers (**NMS 23.7**).

> **UKNS** The UK National Standards for Foster Care also include the following:
>
> - Information on the competences required to be a foster carer (**UKNS 13.4**).
> - That the assessment involves and includes all the carers and others living in the household, their birth children and children they have adopted or fostered (**UKNS 13.5**).
> - That all assessments should be completed within 6 months from the time an application form has been received (**UKNS 13.6**).
> - Prospective carers undergoing an assessment should be encouraged to be actively involved in the process of their assessment and they should be kept up-to-date with the progress and informed of any further work they may need to undertake (**UKNS 13.10**).
> - All prospective carers have a copy of the assessment report (references may be removed) prior to the assessment going to the foster care panel and they should be encouraged to add comments, give further information and attend in order to make any further comments to the panel (**UKNS 13.11**).
> - That they are told of the outcome of the panel and the final decision is sent in writing to them with clear explanations for the decision (**UKNS 13.12**).

What does this mean for you?

Staff who undertake the assessments on behalf of your agency must be qualified and experienced and should have specific experience of family placement work. You will be expected to participate as much as possible in your assessment and some sections of the final report could be written by you, your partner, children or other members of your household/network.

Your agency should have a clear procedure for assessments and note that the UK National Standards state that assessments should be completed within 6 months of your application form being received by the agency.

The assessment process is a very involved piece of work and your agency must keep you informed of the progress and any likely delays in its completion. The process of the assessment is indicated in **NMS 17.7**. Most agencies will use the BAAF Form F or The Fostering Network's assessment forms as the framework of the assessment.

In assessing qualities, competences and aptitudes for fostering, fostering services consider them in relation to the following:

- *child rearing*
- *caring for children born to somebody else*
- *contact between fostered children and their families*
- *helping children make sense of their past*
- *sexual boundaries and attitudes*
- *awareness of issues around child abuse*
- *approaches to discipline*

- awareness of how to promote secure attachments between children and appropriate adults
- awareness of own motivation for fostering/own needs to be met through the fostering process
- religion
- racial/cultural/linguistic issues
- standard of living and lifestyle
- health
- education
- own experience of parenting and being parented
- own experiences in relation to disabilities and/attitudes to disability

NMS 17.7

Your assessor should work out a timetable and schedule of visits to ensure that they are able to see all members of your household and that they are involved in the assessment.

In order to supplement the information above, your assessor will be working with you and your family to gather evidence from other sources that shows you have the necessary skills, knowledge and aptitude to foster. As part of this process you and your family and support network will have to have checks/references undertaken to comply with the *Fostering Services Regulation 2002*.

The checks undertaken on all carers, their household and support networks

There will need to be a consent form signed for every check undertaken to confirm that you agree with and understand the implications of these checks:

- **Police checks:** all adults and children over the age of 18 who are part of the household or who will have frequent and unsupervised contact with foster children will need to be police checked. You will also be expected to identify at least one other person outside your immediate household who will be able to act as part of your support network. They will also be expected to have a police check.
- **Consultancy Index/List 99:** these are registers checked when you have consented to a police check. The lists include all people who are considered to be unsuitable to either work in the caring or educational fields.
- **Local authority check:** this includes checks against the local authority's social services register, probation, child minding, and information that would have been kept by Registration and Inspection Units. These checks are to ensure that you have not been disqualified from working with children or adults.
- **Medicals:** will be undertaken on all the fostering adults/couples. This will give the agency health information on you which would indicate your fitness to foster. Medical information is usually recorded on the BAAF Form AH (Adult Health Report) and this should be filled in by your GP.
  Your medical report will then be sent to the agency's own medical advisor who will make a recommendation about your medical ability to foster. If you are a smoker for instance,

the agency medical advisor may comment on how this may impact on the fostering task and could advise that you do not foster or that you take a certain age range of children only. They will comment in the same manner if you or your partner have other medical complications.

- **Personal references:** at least three personal references are sought on the fostering applicants from people who know them well and who are able to comment on their family life and their ability to care for children. The referees will be visited and a report on the visit will be included in the assessment. Unless specified, these references are kept confidential and will not be shared. The referees will be specifically asked to inform the agency on your ability to care for children safely. Your assessor will need to attach value to each of the referee's comments and this will also be recorded.
- **Work references:** these will be sought on all fostering applicants but especially for those who have worked in the caring or educational fields. They will normally be from line managers of current jobs but could also be from previous employers. If the applicant is in education, a reference will be sent to the course tutor.
 If you have worked in a voluntary capacity where you have had contact with children, references can be sought from the relevant projects.
- **Health and safety check:** this will be undertaken on your home (see Chapter 18 *Safety in the Home*).
- **Safer caring policy for the household:** all households must have one and this should be reviewed regularly so as to minimise risk and keep all family members as well as those in your support network safe (see Chapter 19 *Safer Caring*).

Once your fostering assessment and the accompanying evidence has been completed you will then be shown a copy of the report for any comments and corrections you may wish to suggest. If your assessor disagrees with your suggestions and no agreements can be reached that would satisfy both of you then you will be encouraged to write a supplementary report which will be attached along with the other documents and will go before the fostering panel.

The fostering panel will consider all the information brought before it before making their recommendation. You will also be invited to attend to represent yourself directly (see Chapter 7 *The Fostering Panel*).

Chapter 7

The Fostering Panel

The fostering panel

Fostering panels have clear written policies and procedures, which are implemented in practice, about the handling of their functions.

NMS 30.1

All fostering agencies registered by the Commission for Social Care Inspection are able to set up their own fostering panels and so are able to approve their own carers.

NMS The National Minimum Standards also say the *fostering service* must ensure that:

- There are clear requirements about who can be on the fostering panel. That they must be suitably experienced in childcare and have the required checks undertaken, including a police check before they can take their place on the panel (**NMS 30.3**).
- There is a clear process of decision-making when not all the panel members agree with a position (**NMS 30.2**).
- Fostering panels must have access to medical advice (**NMS 30.4**).
- One of the panel members should be a person who has been in foster care or has had a child placed in foster care (**NMS 30.9**).
- That independent members of the panel should have experience and knowledge in education and in child health (**NMS 30.8**).
- The panel has a clear role in assessing the quality of work brought to panel and should feed back to assessors/the agency details aimed at improving quality, to ensure that there is consistency in the processes of all the reports brought to panel (**NMS 30.5**).
- The fostering panel receives information and updates of all foster care annual reviews (**NMS 30.6**).
- Local authority fostering panels monitor the range of carers available and compare these with the needs of children in foster care or needing to be in foster care (**NMS 30.7**).

> **UKNS** The UK National Standards for Foster Care also include the following:
>
> - That panel members receive training to prepare them for their role on the panel as well as further training aimed at helping them to develop and to enable them to participate fully (**UKNS 23.3**).
> - Comprehensive minutes of the panel discussions are taken and are circulated to all relevant persons including the decision maker and panel members (**UKNS 23.5**).
> - The panel considers the first annual review of carers and any other reviews where significant changes have occurred which will affect the carer's fostering or where there are major concerns regarding the carer's suitability to continue to foster (**UKNS 23.6**).
> - In agencies where all the annual review reports are not presented to the fostering panel, that there is a clear procedure for the re-approval of these reviews and that they are clearly monitored (**UKNS 23.7**).
> - Each carer/potential carer is informed personally of the outcome of the panel and/or the decision maker's decision and that this is followed up in writing (**UKNS 23.9**).
> - That there is a clear protocol and process to appeal against a decision and this is clearly available to carer/potential carer (**UKNS 23.10**).
> - All panel members receive regular management information on the agency, information on the placement needs of the children they look after and are kept up-to-date with important developments, research and examples of good practice (**UKNS 23.11**).
> - That a comprehensive annual report of the work of the panel is produced, this is circulated and is used in discussions for improving the services provided by the agency (**UKNS 23.12**).
> - That the whole panel is involved in the annual report on the fostering service (**UKNS 23.11**).

Fostering panels consists of:
- Not more than 10 people.
- A chair – (needs to be an independent person or someone in the agency with seniority but not responsible for the day to day management of those undertaking the assessments).
- A person designated as vice chair – preferably someone with the same level of independence.
- Two social workers from the agency; one with child care experience and the other with fostering experience.
- A director or a person with responsibility for the agency.

Independent members of the panel:
- A person who is a foster carer for another agency or who has been a foster carer within the previous two years.
- A person experienced in the education of children.
- A person experienced in child health.
- A community representative from the area that the agency is situated in or someone who has been fostered (aged over 18) or a parent of a child who has been in foster care.

Members of the panel can remain on the panel for a period of three years and then for a further three years.

A panel can only be held if it is quorate. This means it has to have the chair or vice chair, one of the agency social workers and at least two of the independent members present.

The role of the panel is to:
- Consider all reports brought to it.
- Recommend the terms of approval i.e. numbers and ages of children, or particular type of fostering the carer can undertake.
- Consider all first annual reviews and subsequent ones especially if there have been major changes or issues for the carers.
- Consider exemptions to the usual fostering limits; where a carer has had a placement outside the terms of approval.
- Hear cases of allegations and complaints against carers.
- Consider reports for the termination of a carer's approval.
- Advise and offer guidance on issues of standards and quality for the assessing and supporting of foster carers.
- Advise and offer guidance to the agency as appropriate.

Panel recommendations

The panel has to make clear recommendations to the agency decision maker (normally the Director or Chief Executive), who will ultimately need to make the final decision. The decision maker will have had access to *all* the information and can overturn the recommendation of the panel or vary the details of the recommendations put forward.

The outcome from the panel and the decision maker should be conveyed both verbally and in writing as soon as is possible.

What does this mean for you?

Most agency panels should welcome your attendance both when you come for your initial approval or for the presentation of your annual review. Your supervising social worker should help you to prepare for this. It can be daunting to enter a room where there can be up to ten people waiting to see you, however, it is a clear responsibility of any panel, especially the chair, to make your attendance as comfortable as possible. Ask your supervising social worker for the agency procedures about applicants and carers attending panel – they should have one.

Usually a panel will be able to make its recommendation once they have looked at all evidence brought before it and they have asked their questions. Some panels may be able to say immediately what they are recommending and the details. This can be even if they will not be able to recommend your approval/re-approval. It is ultimately the agency decision maker who will make the final decision and confirm approval details. These will then be sent to you in writing. If the decision maker decides not to approve or re-approve then you will be given details of how to appeal and you will have 28 days to do so. For further details see Chapter 31 *Termination of Approval*.

Chapter 8

The Foster Care Agreement

The Foster Care Agreement

Foster Care Agreements ensure foster carers have a full understanding of what is expected of foster carers, the agency and/or the local authority.

In producing the Foster Care Agreement for a foster carer, in line with Schedule 5 of the Fostering Services Regulations 2002, the fostering provider ensures that the Agreement contains the information they need to know, in a comprehensible style, to carry out their functions as a foster carer effectively.

NMS 22.2 and 22.4

What the regulations say

Schedule 5 says the Foster Care Agreement must contain the following:

- That a carer must '…care for any child as if the child were a member of the foster parent's family and to promote their welfare having regard to the long and short-term plans for the child' (Schedule 5.11).
- The terms of your approval – the approval category made by the decision maker of your fostering agency, ie how many children you may be able to foster, their ages, etc.
- Information about the support and training you are to be given by your agency.
- The procedure for your re-approval.
- The procedure for the placing of children by the agency.
- Details of what is to be included in the foster placement agreement (Schedule 6 – see Appendix 1).
- How you and the agency are covered under any legal liabilities from fostering.
- Details and procedures of how you can make a complaint or get your views across.
- That you must give written notification to your agency if:
  - You change address or if you move.
  - Your household composition changes.
  - There are any changes in your circumstances that affect your ability or your suitability to care.
  - You make a request or an application to adopt or you are registered as a child minder or registered to provide day care.
- That under no circumstances should you administer corporal punishment to children in your care.
- That all the information relating to children in your care, their family or any other person connected to the child is kept strictly confidential and not disclosed to anyone unless with the agreement of the fostering service.

- That all carers must work with and uphold the foster placement agreement (as set out in Schedule 6) see *Appendix 1 – Foster Placement Agreement*.
- How to work within the fostering agency's policies and procedures especially with regard to child protection and managing difficult behaviour in children.
- How to co-operate with the Commission for Social Care Inspection and to allow persons authorised by the Commission, as part of their role in inspecting fostering services, to visit you at your home and interview you.
- How to ensure that you keep your agency and the child's local authority informed about the child's progress and to notify them of any changes which affect or will affect the child.
- How to allow a child who is placed with you to be removed from your home (Reg 36).

Schedule 5 of the Fostering Regulations 2002 makes provisions for when the placement is considered no longer suitable for the child or young person or where to continue the placement would be in the child or young person's detriment.

What does this mean for you?

All carers should be given a copy of the Foster Care Agreement to keep and refer to. This agreement outlines the requirements laid out in the Fostering Services Regulations 2002. It is very important that you understand what is contained in this agreement as it sets out what your agency expects of you and what you can expect from your agency. Your supervising social worker will normally ask you to sign a copy for your file which is kept in the office. You should also keep your own copy safe.

It is likely that your foster care agreement may contain information other than those listed above. Your agency may have specific policies for instance about smoking or how the fostering allowances are to be spent, and will use the foster care agreement to convey the weight it puts on the matter. However, no foster care agreement can cover *all* the areas. You will need to consider your foster care agreement along with other policies and procedure; instructions and guidance given to you by your agency or the child's local authority and these would usually be in a foster care manual you should receive from your agency.

What is the difference between being approved by the fostering panel and the Foster Care Agreement?

- Your *approval* is the confirmation that you can foster and is confirmed by the agency's decision-maker. This contains details of the approval category for the year and can change from year to year depending upon your capacity to foster and your availability. Your agency will confirm your approval in writing.
- Your *Foster Care Agreement* is the agreement that you sign with your agency – like a work contract and contains the information listed above. This is given to you when you begin to foster.

Chapter 9

Terms and Conditions for Foster Carers

Terms and conditions for fosters carers

The fostering service is a fair and competent employer, with sound employment practices and good support for its staff and carers.

NMS 18.1

As with most jobs, carers have their own terms and conditions. The Foster Care Agreement is the written contract; the task description can be seen as the job description and the competencies can be seen as the job specification (see Chapter 8 *The Foster Care Agreement* and Chapter 5 *Recruiting Carers*).

The specific conditions of *your* service are contained in the Foster Care Agreement you sign with your agency.

NMS The National Minimum Standards also say the *fostering service* must ensure that:

- You understand the nature of your Foster Care Agreement and are clear about the expectations placed upon you, your agency and the local authority (**NMS 22.2**) and that the Foster Care Agreement contains all the information you need, in a clearly written style to enable you to carry out your role as a foster carer well (**NMS 22.4**).
- That you have a named supervising social worker who works with you and who has the necessary qualifications and access to the wider professional support network to enable them to provide you and the young person with consistent and high quality support (**NMS 22.3**).
- That your supervising social worker meets with you on a regular basis and that these meetings have a clear purpose (**NMS 22.6**).
- That you will have at least one unannounced visit a year (**NMS 22.6**).
- That once you have been approved, you are given a handbook which contains all the policies, procedures, guidance, legal information and insurance details to enable you to carry out your tasks as a carer and that these are updated regularly (**NMS 22.5**).
- Your agency should have a written policy on the fostering allowance/payments and these should be available freely and given to carers on a yearly basis (**NMS 29.2**). Your allowances/payments should be made to you promptly (**NMS 22.7**).
- That the information about fostering allowances/payments contains details on how this should be spent for each child placed (**NMS 29.2**).

→

- The fees and expenses you receive reflect the cost and nature of the fostering you are undertaking (**NMS 29.1**).
- That training and support is offered to sons and daughters of foster carers (**NMS 23.7**) and specific training is provided on safe caring for all members of the household (**NMS 23.6**).
- You have access to 24 hour support (**NMS 18.3, 21.2, 22.7**).
- Your agency has arrangements for when children are not in education (**NMS 13.7**).
- Your agency has adequate insurance cover including public liability and professional indemnity for all its carers and employees and that this specifically covers costs that may arise as a result of a child abuse claim (**NMS 18.6** and **22.7**). That your agency also has a comprehensive health and safety policy and this too covers all legal requirements (**NMS 18.5**).
- Your agency has a whistle blowing policy which is easy to understand and use (**NMS 18.7**). (See Chapter 32 Whistle-blowing).

UKNS The UK National Standards in Foster Care also include the following:

- That the fostering agency positively encourages and supports the carers' own support networks (**UKNS 14.12**).
- That fostering agencies conduct exit interviews when a carer is planning to leave the agency to see what can be learned from the foster carers' experiences of working for that agency (**UKNS 21.11**).

As stated above, it is important that you link the information in the Foster Care Agreement, your agency handbook or manual, the job or task description and competencies to get the full picture of your terms and conditions.

Chapter 10

Supervision and Support

Supervision/support/advice/information

The fostering service has a clear strategy for working with and supporting carers.

Each approved foster carer is supervised by a named, appropriately qualified social worker and has access to adequate social work and other professional support, information and advice to enable her/him to provide consistent, high quality care for a child or young person placed in her or his home. The supervising social worker ensures each carer she or he supervises is informed in writing of, and accepts, understands and operates within, all standards, policies and guidance agreed by the fostering service.

NMS 21.1 and 22.3

NMS The National Minimum Standards also say the *fostering service* must ensure that:

- All foster carers receive a foster care agreement and this contains information on what is expected of foster carers, the agency and the local authority (**NMS 22.2**) and that it is written in a clear and readable way and contains all the information carers need to know to carry out their tasks as a carer effectively (**NMS 22.4**).
- That all carers are given a handbook which contains all the policies, procedures, guidance, legal information as well as insurance details and that the handbook is regularly updated (**NMS 22.5**).
- That supervising social workers meet with carers on a regular basis for supervision and that these meetings have a clear aim. That all supervision is recorded and a copy is kept on the carer's office file. Occasional unannounced visits (at least once a year) are undertaken and these too are recorded and filed (**NMS 22.6**).
- Practical support offered to carers include out of office hours support, payments to carers being made promptly, adequate insurance cover for the fostering role, support for them to take part in fostering groups/associations, the provision of respite care and access to a range of social work support (**NMS 22.7**). Further support includes clear plans to offer carers training and development opportunities, access to information and advice, support and assistance in dealing with other services, e.g. health and education, support and information about the carers' annual review process and especially clarity regarding the role of supervision between carers and their supervising social worker (**NMS 21.2**).

→

- That carers are informed about the policy and procedure for complaints and representations (**NMS 22.8**).
- That carers are informed about the policy and procedure for allegations against carers, that they are entitled to the support of an independent person through such an investigation (**NMS 22.9**), that the carer has clear information about the circumstances that could lead to their name being removed from the foster carer register (**NMS 22.10**) See *Appendix 2 Foster Care Register*.

Issues regarding the supervision, support, advice and information to carers are encompassed in all the chapters of this guide and too numerous to reproduce here. The agency responsibility ranges from the details needed to satisfy their Statement of Purpose as set out in **NMS 1** (See Appendix 3 *Statement of Purpose*) to the provision in **NMS 18.2**, that all fostering agencies have 'sound employment practices, in relation to both staff and carers'.

What does this mean for you?

Supervision is an important aspect of the relationship between you and your supervising social worker and is a much encouraged component of the Code of Practice in Foster Care as well as in the National Minimum Standards and the UK National Standards.

Supervision should help to formalise the relationship between you and your supervising social worker and should ensure that relevant information on you, your household and the young people in placement are covered and recorded. You should be given a copy of the supervision reports which you should check and sign. Be aware that you too can record aspects and especially the occasions and the reasons why you may not agree with your supervising social worker about any particular aspect of the discussions. These records will also be considered as evidence of work you have undertaken and of the development of your fostering skills and be considered at your annual foster care review.

Prior to beginning supervision, your supervising social worker should discuss with you the supervision 'contract' (**NMS 22.6**). Information contained in it should include:

- Frequency of contact you can expect from your supervising social worker, both in terms of visits, attending meetings and by phone (**NMS 22.6**).
- The time span of meetings and where you are to meet.
- Who should attend the meeting; your supervising social worker may want to see your partner, children, people from your support network etc.
- A regular look at the handbook which contains advice and information about acceptable practice and procedures and feed back from this should inform the necessary updates and improvements in the overall service provided by the agency (**NMS 20.2** and **22.5**).
- The information or resources you may require to meet the needs of your placement. Your supervising social worker may be able to offer this information or resource directly or may enable you to be in touch with 'experts' who can advise you on matters such as education, health, legal, child care, culture, language etc (**NMS 16.13**).

- A regular review of your fostering skills and competencies which would then be compiled for your annual foster care review.
- Regular reviewing of the child care plans to see if you are able to meet the young person's needs.
- Training; both a discussion of training received and training required.
- Updates on any changes in law or regulations which may affect the fostering task (**NMS 19.4**).
- Health and safety; your supervising social worker will periodically need to check your household to see if there are any health and safety issues in line with your agency's health and safety policy (**NMS 18.5**). They will also need to see the young person's room and to be satisfied that the young person has enough privacy if they want it and have sufficient quiet space to do homework/undertake leisure activities that are home based.
- Contact issues; any difficulties should be discussed and strategies agreed for resolving them.
- Complaints or allegations; this is a clear place to discuss these issues fully (**NMS 22.8** and **22.9**).

This is not an exhaustive list. You will need to discuss the necessary and individual issues about your family and the young person in placement. Remember, the aim of supervision is for it to be useful and an aid to learning. There may be some times, however, when you may agree to abandon the set format and just let the conversation flow. What is important, however, is that you have useful discussions which help you with the tasks at hand. You should still get a copy of the discussions.

Your supervising social worker should, of course, ensure that you receive all the relevant information about the young person you are caring for.

Also at the beginning of your relationship with your supervising social worker you will be reminded that it is part of the regulations (Volume 3, The Children Act 1989) that your supervising social worker should undertake at least one unannounced visit per year (**NMS 22.6**). This means that your supervising social worker can turn up at any time and unless it is exceptionally inconvenient you should let them in. These visits could be 'routine' or could be in response to a complaint or a concern they may have about you, members of your household or the young person you are caring for. You should always be given adequate information *whatever* the reason for the visit. Your supervising social worker will have specific responsibilities if there is a child protection enquiry going on (see Chapter 20 *Child Protection*).

There is also a range of practical support offered to you by your agency and your supervising social worker – see Chapter 9 *Terms and Conditions for Foster Carers*.

The role of the young person's social worker

Each child or young person placed in foster care has a designated social worker who ensures statutory requirements for her/his care and protection are met and promotes her or his welfare and development.

> **UKNS** The UK National Standards in Foster Care say the following:
>
> - That each child looked after in foster care should have a social worker who is professionally qualified in aspects of child care and has the experience to work with children in foster care (**UKNS 5.1**) and that the social worker visits the child regularly, alone and with the carer, at least within the statutory requirements for visits and any other times as may be set out in the placement agreement (**UKNS 5.7**).
> - That the care plan for the child contains the name of their social worker and details changes of social worker and reasons for the change (**UKNS 5.2**).
> - That the social worker is clearly identified to the child, their family and the foster carer and they all know what the social worker's responsibilities are and how to contact them (**UKNS 5.3**).
> - That the caseload of the social worker is such that there is time for them to work fully with the child, their family and the foster carer towards effecting the child's care plan (**UKNS 5.4**) and the social worker is responsible for monitoring and recording the progress made including liaising with other professionals linked into the care plan (**UKNS 5.6**).
> - That the social worker is responsible for providing any specialist support or resources the child may need (**UKNS 5.5**).
> - That the social worker is responsible for managing contact as set out in the care plan and ensures that the child is kept in touch with events happening to their family or to important people in their lives (**UKNS 5.8**).
> - That there are clear arrangements in place to ensure during periods when the social worker may be absent, that there is someone else to contact for advice and support and that this information is known to all involved with the child (**UKNS 5.9**).

Depending on which local authority has placed the child or young person, the social worker may be local or from another part of the country. This should not make a difference to the service the child receives from their social worker who should make the same number of visits, keep in regular contact by telephone and organise and attend meetings and the child's reviews (see Chapter 5). Foster carers have a crucial role in helping to prepare a child for their social worker's visit and enabling them to have the time and space to talk.

When they visit, the social worker will want to talk to you but they will also need to spend time alone with the child and look at their bedroom. They are also obliged under the Children Act Regulations to make unannounced visits. Working in partnership with the child's social worker is crucial to the success of any placement and helps everyone involved to remain focussed on the best interests of the child.

It is always difficult to define clearly the differences in the roles of your supervising social worker and the role of the young person's social worker especially when it is to do with the needs of the young person. However, some activities define the roles more clearly. Below is an outline of what each does – this is not exhaustive. Significantly, however, it is important to note that both your supervising social worker and the young person's social worker should promote the health and well being of the young person and both should support you in your endeavours to achieve this *and* the expectations placed on you. Quite often you will find that in the absence of the young person's allocated social worker, your supervising social worker will undertake some of these responsibilities.

The role of the young person's social worker is to:

- Take responsibility for the welfare and supervision of the young person.
- Undertake direct work with the young person including ensuring that the young person's personal education plan (PEP – see Chapter 23) is triggered off by the school *and* that their health needs are met.
- Maintain links for the young person with their birth family and those significant to them. In some cases they will be able to help in the tracing of birth parents or significant people.
- Work with birth parents towards the rehabilitation of their children back to them or where this is not the plan to help make positive moves for the young person to move on.
- Liaise with foster carers and gain information on how the young person is doing in foster care and make sure all the points agreed at the child's review are carried out.
- Make sure the young person has got adequate clothing and possessions to enable them to move into foster care.
- Ensure that plans for the young person are made, progressed and reviewed and all the necessary work and forms are completed.

The role of the supervising social worker

> *The role of the supervising social worker is clear both to the worker and to the carer. Visits are regular and properly recorded. Annual review reports are prepared and are available to the Fostering Panel.*
>
> **NMS 21.5**

The role of the supervising social worker is to:

- Recruit, assess, train and support foster carers.
- Provide supervision to carers and using a range of methods enable carers to develop their competencies.
- Ensure that foster carers are matched with children they are equipped and skilled to care for.
- Provide the wide range of support necessary to enable foster carers to know what is expected of them within the child/young person's care plan and enable them to meet these expectations both practically and emotionally.
- Review foster carers annually or more frequently if necessary and make recommendation together with the foster carer as to their re-approval category.
- Support foster carers when they are the subject of a complaint or an allegation and to provide them with clear information about the process and other areas in which they may obtain support and information.
- Participate in the planning for the young person.
- Help carers prepare the young person to move in to and out of their household.
- Attend meetings jointly with the foster carer on the young person or to represent/advocate on behalf of the young person or foster carer.

Support groups

Most agencies run a monthly support group for foster carers which they should attend regularly although there will inevitably be times when placements, illness or other difficulties might prevent you from doing so. Foster carers' support groups are an excellent opportunity for foster carers to share experiences and support one another. Often, support groups will have a particular topic to discuss and carers find that it helps to talk over a problem or difficulty with other foster carers who may well have found a way to resolve it.

Support carers/support network

Your support network consists of the people you have identified during the assessment stage and since, who you would call on for support while you are fostering. It is both necessary to identify these people and to ensure that you review this position regularly so that when an emergency arises and you have to rely on your support network, then they are still available. You would not normally call upon your support network to undertake regular aspects of your fostering responsibilities but they can be people who will offer you or your own children time out.

Your support network will have undergone a range of statutory checks because they are likely to have 'substantial and unsupervised contact' with a young person you are caring for. Anyone else who is also likely to have 'substantial and unsupervised contact' with a young person but who may not be offering practical help will also need to be checked.

As with the checks on yourself and members of your family over 18 years of age, these will need to be renewed three yearly. For further information about the checks see Chapter 6 *Assessing Carers*.

Aspects of your support network and how they relate to you and any child in placement will be one of the areas covered in your annual foster care review. Remember that your support network may not be as able or as committed to young children as you are, especially after a particularly difficult placement, and may decide that they can no longer offer any help. It is important not to over stretch the help of some of these supporters so if you can identify a few different people, then this could help prevent difficulties.

If you find yourself in a position where you cannot identify any specific support, you should discuss this with your supervising social worker. However, it is part of Competency 4.2 to have:

An ability to have people and links within the community which provide support.

Your agency should also provide opportunities for your support network to attend training, support groups and other related activities.

Chapter 11

Training

Training

The fostering service ensures that foster carers are trained in the skills required to provide high quality care and meet the needs of each child/young person placed in their care.

NMS 23.1

NMS The National Minimum Standards specifically indicates that training is given on the following:

- Health and safety (**NMS 6.7**).
- Enhancing the young person's confidence and feeling of self worth (**NMS 7.3**) and boosting and maintaining self-esteem (**NMS 9.2**).
- The young person's ethnic, religious, cultural and linguistic background (**NMS 7.4**) and that training stresses the importance of contact for the child (**NMS 10.5**).
- Anti-discrimination and how to help young people (**NMS 7.5**).
- Equal opportunities (**NMS 23.3**).
- Transracial or transcommunity placements and understanding a young person's heritage (**NMS 8.6**).
- Safe caring skills, managing behaviour and recognising signs of abuse (**NMS 9.2**) for all the fostering household (**NMS 23.6**).
- Recording and encouraging young people to record significant life events (**NMS 24.7**).
- Life history work (**NMS 24.7**).
- Health promotion (see Chapter 21 *Children's Health*), hygiene and first aid (**NMS 12.5**).
- Helping a young person to leave care and in to independent living (**NMS 14.3**).
- Policies and procedures in foster care that reflect the service offered by your agency (**NMS 19.6**).
- Specific training as appropriate to sons and daughters of foster carers and their extended network and support networks (**NMS 23.7**).
- An on-going programme of training designed to develop skills and tackle any challenging issues carers may have (**NMS 23.5**) plus the opportunity to undertake post approval qualification such as NVQ (**NMS 19.2**).
- That there is regular joint training with staff (**NMS 19.7**).
- Attention is given to the training needs of particular groups, e.g. male carers (**NMS 23.4**).
- Prospective carers should have the opportunities to meet with existing carers during the induction and pre-approval training and all new carers receive induction training (**NMS 23.2**).

- Where a member of a child's family or friendship network is wanting to care for the child, all the above training opportunities are to be given to them also (**NMS 32.3**).

What does this mean for you?

As you will see from this guide, training is a central and intrinsic part of fostering and all agencies must have a clear plan for the training and development of all who work in the service (**NMS 19.2**). There are also clear expectations that carers will participate in the training offered by their agency as fully as possible. The lack of take up of training could influence continued approval as a carer and will be something that is taken up at the annual review. All training offered must be within an equal opportunities and anti-discriminatory framework (**NMS 23.3**).

The training you undertake will be recorded on a training portfolio, which will be kept on your file and will be used as part of your annual review (**NMS 16.9**). Your supervising social worker will talk to you about the formulation of your own personal portfolio in which your training needs for the coming 12 months will be indicated. This will normally be done during your supervision time with your supervising social worker or could be done through the appraisal system. All agencies must operate appraisal systems for all their staff and including foster carers is conducive to good practice (**NMS 19.3**). A new 12-month plan should be compiled for your annual review along with comments about learning (**NMS 23.8**).

Apart from the individual work with your supervising social worker, you will also have opportunities to make suggestions for training topics. Your agency needs to be able to offer training at different times and at different places to enable you, your partner and any other members of your family (where appropriate) to attend training. Your agency should also try to provide child care where there is a clear difficulty of making child care arrangements and without which the carer(s) would not be able to attend the training. Reasonable expenses incurred in coming to the training should be met by the agency (**NMS 23.3**).

Your feed back on the training offered will also be sought as your agency should be undertaking regular evaluations and reviews of the quality and usefulness of the training they have provided (**NMS 19.5**). The outcomes of these should be conveyed to all carers (**NMS 23.9**).

Where there are two adults within the household who are being assessed jointly, then both should undertake all mandatory training (**NMS 23.4**) and your agency should make what they consider to be 'mandatory' training clear to you.

Chapter 12

Listening to and Involving Children

A child's right to be listened to

The fostering service ensures that children's opinions and those of their families and others significant to the child, are sought over all issues which are likely to affect their daily life and their future.

NMS 11

> **NMS** The National Minimum Standards also say the *fostering service* must ensure that children and young people:
>
> - Have their opinions sought not just for important decisions in their life but routine and daily issues (**NMS 11.1; 11.3**).
> - Are not to be taken for granted and nor should their opinions be ignored (**NMS 11.3**).
> - Should be provided with 'suitable means' which would enable them to easily express their opinions and allow them to overcome any communication difficulties they may have so that they can be 'frequently' given the opportunity to be involved (**NMS 11.4**).
> - Know how to raise concerns and complaints and that those caring for them promote this right (**NMS 11.5**).
> - Should receive *prompt* feedback once complaints or concerns have been made (**NMS 11.5**).

In recognition of the crucial role that you and your family would play in 'listening', 'hearing' and 'responding' to the child, there are requirements placed on your agency to ensure that you receive the necessary training and are supported to facilitate this crucial right to the children you care for (**NMS 11.2**) (see *Introduction*, and *Appendix 4*).

Chapter 13

Valuing the Diversity of the Child

Valuing diversity

The fostering service ensures that children and young people, and their families, are provided with foster care services which value diversity and promote equality.

NMS 7.1

NMS The National Minimum Standards also say the *fostering service* must ensure that:

- The fostering service is one that values and helps to promote for the child and their family, their religion, ethnic origin, language, culture, disability, sexuality and their gender (**NMS 7.2**).
- They ensure that carers 'respect and preserve' each child's ethnic, religious, cultural and linguistic heritage and that this is also reinforced within training for carers both at the preparation stage and then at later stages (**NMS 7.4**).
- If a placement is made in an emergency and aspects of the above list are not matched, then the fostering service has 6 weeks to address these and decide on further action (**NMS 7.2**).
- Both the fostering service and children's social workers work together to enhance the child's confidence and self-esteem and that this is another of the areas that training is provided for foster carers and social workers (**NMS 7.3**).
- Their foster carers help and encourage each child to develop the skills to deal with all forms of discrimination and that this is also a subject of training for the carer (**NMS 7.5**).
- Their foster carers encourage each child and enable access to opportunities that will help develop and or pursue their interests, talents and hobbies. That fostering agencies set this out in written information for their foster carers (**NMS 7.7**).
- Children with disabilities are provided with the services and supports which will enable them to access as wide a range of activities as possible (**NMS 7.7**) to maximise their potential and help them to live as full a life as possible. This should include the appropriate equipment and adaptation within their home and/or their vehicle (**NMS 7.6**).

UKNS The UK National Standards for Foster Care also include the following:

- Taking into account the age and the child's ability to understand that each child/young person has a right to be fully involved with the decisions taken about their lives and the care that they are given. That they be provided with advocacy and other support to ensure they are able to fully participate and exercise their rights (**UKNS 1.7**).

What does this mean for you?

Valuing diversity within your home

Local authorities look to place children into families that match their needs. These placements need to consider not only the young person's ethnicity, religion, language but their culture and traditions as well as issues of disability, sexuality and gender (**NMS 7.2; 7.4**). This is a very complex set of matching considerations and one that is not going to be always easy to match. Even when a young person's ethnic background is matched there may be other elements that are not met or run contrary to the young person's heritage.

What fostering agencies are expecting and looking for from their carers is their ability to consider the needs of a young person and to assist in finding ways to bridge any gaps. As a carer, although you will receive support and advice from the young person's social worker and your supervising social worker, you will be expected to do your own research to expand your knowledge. You will need to become familiar with the young person's background and heritage so you can actively promote the customs and culture and maintain a good sense of identity for the young person. You will be expected to have a good understanding of how racism impacts on our society and how it might do so on the child or young person you are caring for.

It is vital that you are able to establish good working relationships with the young person's parents or anyone else from their background as they will be able to give you first hand information necessary to the young person. If this is not possible, get in touch with community groups, seek information from the Internet, from books, anywhere! Don't forget, you can ask the young person. Show an active interest on your own behalf and get your family involved.

Equally important is to be up front about not knowing everything but being open enough to learning and to actively pursue avenues that will increase the quality of life for the young people you look after.

Your fostering agency may ask you to take a child or young person in an emergency knowing that the match for the young person is not the best choice. There is provision in the standards that the young person can stay with you for up to six weeks which should allow either a more suitable placement to be found or resources to be identified and provided that may make the placement more suitable (**NMS 7.2**).

As mentioned above, the process of making suitable matches for children and young people is very complicated. Other equally important factors include the ability of the carers to keep the child's family ties vibrant and positive, help children to build confidence in themselves and work on their sense of self worth (**NMS 7.3**). With regard to children with learning difficulties or disabilities, this is especially an issue. There is a clear acknowledgement that children should be provided with the services and supports which help to make them as independent as possible and helps them to lead as full a life as possible (**NMS 7.6**). Carers are expected, as with all the children they care for, to create opportunities for children/young people that will help to develop and pursue their talents and hobbies (**NMS 7.7**).

Many of the standards in this section underline the necessity for carers to be provided with training. An essential training requirement is assisting carers to encourage each child to develop skills enabling them to deal with all the forms of discrimination they may face (**NMS 7.5**).

Chapter 14

Children Being Placed With You

Matching children into your home

Local authority fostering services, and voluntary agencies placing children in their own right, ensure that each child or young person placed in foster care is carefully matched with a carer capable of meeting her/his assessed needs. For agencies providing foster carers to local authorities, those agencies ensure that they offer carers only if they represent appropriate matches for a child for whom a local authority is seeking a carer.

NMS 8.1

> **NMS** The National Minimum Standards also say the *fostering service* must ensure that:
>
> - The process of matching children with carers must consider aspects in the child's care plan as well as any other assessments undertaken on the child, the child's family as well as the carer and the carer's family (**NMS 8.2**).
> - All the information necessary with which to make a match is shared with relevant professionals and that the matching of a child into a placement is undertaken once this information is shared. This includes obtaining the views of the child, their family, the potential carer, their family and other children in placement (**NMS 8.3**).
> - The matching process includes the matching in areas such as race, ethnicity, religion, culture and language (**NMS 8.5**).
> - The foster placement agreement contains the reasons for a placement and identifies the gaps and the additional support and resources to be provided to fill the gaps to make the placement more compatible (**NMS 8.4**) Where a placement is made outside the child's community or where there is not a match on the grounds of race, culture etc, the agencies involved should provide the carer with further training, support and information so that they can offer the best possible care by having a clear understanding of the child's heritage (**NMS 8.6**). However, where a placement is made as an emergency and the placement is not a suitable match, then steps to achieve a better match need to be taken within 6 weeks (**NMS 7.2**). This can mean that the child's placement is a bridging one only, pending a more suitable match.
> - Each child has the opportunity to meet with their potential carer in advance so they can form their own views on the placement and also prepare for the move. They should be introduced to the carer and their family, any other children that may be living there, see the home, meet family pets and get some idea about the neighbourhood before moving in (**NMS 8.7**).
>
> →

- If the child to be placed has been abused or has abused another child, then a full assessment should be made not just on that child but on all other children in the household prior to any decision about sharing a bedroom. The outcome of the assessment must be recorded (**NMS 6.5**).
- The relationship a child has to members of their family or where a child has a significant friendship, should be recognised and considered when looking for a placement (**NMS 32.2**); and that the process for assessing and approving such carers is done with sensitivity and encouragement (**NMS 32.4**); and that *their* needs for support and training are met in the same way as for other carers (**NMS 32.3**).

UKNS The UK National Standards for Foster Care also include the following:

- That priority is given to enabling siblings to remain together, if this has been assessed to be in their best interests (**UKNS 4.8**).
- That there is a placement report written at the end of each placement so that necessary lessons can be learnt for any future placement for the child and for those particular carers (**UKNS 4.12**).

What does this mean for you?

When a child is to be placed into your home, all those involved in the process must be satisfied that it is the best match possible. If the matching considerations fall short, then there is a responsibility on all those involved with the child to identify and meet the needs. When planning for placements, you should have had discussions about your needs and the needs of your *own* children as well as other children you may be fostering. Your own family will have their own particular issues and characteristics and while these will have been assessed with you during the preparation period, they may have changed. As has been indicated, matching is a complicated process and this is where the skill of your agency's staff will come into play.

Other aspects important to the matching considerations are highlighted in Chapter 12 *Listening to and Involving Children* and Chapter 13 *Valuing the Diversity of the Child*. This includes the child's racial, ethnic, religious, cultural and linguistic needs and the potential match in these areas to that of the foster carer and their family (**NMS 8.5**).

Where gaps in the matching process are identified, this should be noted in the placement planning meeting and plans made for bridging the gaps (**NMS 8.4**). There should be a placement planning meeting (see Chapter 15) at the time of the placement or ideally this should be done in advance. The meeting should be attended by the foster carers, the child, the child's parents (if appropriate), the child's social worker and your supervising social worker.

In order to maximise the chances of a placement succeeding, it *is* good practice to share information with all the professionals involved. Your agency should share information about *you and your family* with the child's placing authority. They should be sent a copy of your assessment report and any other recent documents or assessments, such as your foster care review, to the local authority who will need to agree the placement and match in advance.

There should be an introduction for the child and a meeting in advance of the placement is considered good practice (**NMS 8.7**). This is where you can then begin to get to know the young person, show them round, introduce them to your own children, your pets, show them toys you have etc. During your preparation stage, your supervising social worker should have discussed with you the preparation of a family photo album which would be a pleasant and friendly way of introducing your family to the young person, especially if they cannot be at the meeting with you. Remember that such a meeting should have as much information shared about you, as it should be about you getting information about the young person. Young people are likely to be extremely nervous, angry, frightened, or a combination of all and more. Think ahead to what it may be like for the child. Ensure the beginning of a young person's placement is as pleasant as possible.

By the placement planning meeting, you should already have written information on the child (see Chapter 15 *Looked After Documents*). Within these documents you will find the medical consent to enable the child or young person to be medically treated while they are with you. It is vital that you are given the consent which the child's parent will have signed enabling you to register the child with a GP, dentist etc. as well as to follow up on-going treatment. If the child is on a care order (see Chapter 15 *Looked After Documents*) then the local authority will give the consent.

If a meeting in advance of the placement is not possible, then your agency should ensure that the child's social worker telephones and discusses the placement needs, aims and care plan for the child in advance of the placement.

Where a carer has another child in place, your agency should consult with the social worker for that child and inform them as fully as possible what the implications might be.

At the beginning of a placement, all children should be given a copy of the various agencies *Children's Guides*. These guides should contain information about what a child can expect from a foster placement as well as from their social worker. It should also give clear information should they wish to make comments about their care or if they wish to make a complaint.

What should I do when preparing for a placement?

Some things to consider:

- Check the state of the young person's bedroom – will they have sufficient play and study space?
- Is the layout and decoration of the room/home suitable – perhaps some quick touches may be possible to make it more inviting or you may be able to speak to the young person who could be involved in choosing different paint colours, for instance. Or just a new set of bedding may do it.
- Look at the books, toys and other items you have and check that they are safe and that they reflect the multi-racial, multi-cultural society we live in.
- Is your family album up to date?

What authority do I have to look after children/young people?

Legally a young person is looked after in two different ways; either with their parent's consent or without it. If consent has been given 'voluntarily', then the parents can also remove their child from care without the permission of social services and they have a right to do so at any time. The young person in these circumstances would be 'accommodated'. The 1989 Children Act looks to develop the partnership between the local authority and the parent for the best interests of the young person. Where it is possible to have good co-operation, the law encourages not to get the courts involved.

Where the parent(s) may not have given consent and an order is given in the court, this is called a **care order** or an **interim care order**. The latter would be given for a specified period after which the case would go back to the court for a final decision about the future of the child or young person. In these circumstances the parents will still have their parental rights (parental responsibility) but this will be shared with the local authority.

There are two other types of orders:

- **Emergency Protection Order (EPO):** this is an order given by the courts when it is essential to keep a child away from their home in an emergency. This order can last up to 28 days but can be less. The court will need to be convinced that the child is 'suffering or likely to suffer from significant harm' immediately if action is not taken. This order gives parental responsibility to the local authority who will share it with the child's parents but the responsibility mainly rests with the local authority.
- **Police Protection Order (PPO):** this order allows the police to take a child/young person away from the scene where the police believe that a child may be at risk or likely to be and take them to a hospital, a police station or to a foster home. This order lasts up to 72 hours and gives the local authority time to carry out an assessment of the risk the child may be in. The order would need to be extended by the local authority at court if they believed the child to be at risk if they were to be returned home.

What if parents want to remove their child from my home?

You may find yourself in the position where a parent turns up at your door wanting their child back. If a child is accommodated (i.e. in care voluntarily) then their parents still retain the right to take their children back. In these circumstances you should immediately inform your agency and the local authority but you may not stop the child from being taken away. The only exception would be if you feel the young person would be put in danger, i.e. if the parent turns up drunk for instance. Then you may have to call the police immediately if you cannot persuade them to leave the young person with you.

If the young person is on a care order or an interim care order, an Emergency Protection Order or a Police Protection Order, then no one is allowed to take the child away from you without agreement by the local authority while the order is in force. Different orders have different time limits and you must be aware of this. If parents do remove their child while the order is in force, then you must notify the authority and the police that you have been unable to persuade the parent to leave the child with you. You should have been given a copy of the child's court order by the local authority.

Chapter 15

Looked After Children Documents

Children's documents

Children are matched with carers taking into account the child's care plan and recent written assessment of the child and their family and the carers.

NMS 8.2

A written care plan is prepared for each child or young person placed in foster care; all aspects of the plan are implemented, it is reviewed regularly and any changes are made only as a result of a review meeting.

UKNS 3

An up-to-date comprehensive case record is maintained for each child or young person in foster care which details the nature and quality of care provided and contributes to an understanding of her/his life events; relevant information from the case record is made available to the child and to anyone involved in her/his care.

UKNS 8

The Integrated Children's System (ICS) was developed from the findings of two government initiatives – (a) the Assessment Framework and (b) the Looked After Children (LAC) documents. The ICS provides a single and comprehensive system of recording information and planning for children and their families and replaces the Assessment Framework and the LAC documentation. The uniformity of these materials means that if a young person and their family move to other parts of the country, then there should be an accessible record of the young person which can be readily shared and readily available in a compatible way, including on computer.

One of the drawbacks with the previous initiatives was the inability to readily store and share vital information with other professions, both within the same locality and those at some distance. This can now be rectified.

The Integrated Children's System documentation is given to you as a carer when a child or young person is placed with you or in some cases during the planning stage. These papers should provide all the information on the young person and enable the child or young person's progress to be planned and reviewed effectively. Get to know the range of documentation so that you can check you have all the relevant forms for the child or young person you are caring for.

There are four parts to the Integrated Children's System:

- information
- assessment
- planning
- reviewing

Information documents

1. **Contact Record:** this is an enquiry form and is used to record all the enquiries made by or on behalf of a child and their family and will record briefly what action was taken or outcome of the enquiry.

2. **Referral and Information Record:** this is used to gather essential information about the child or young person and their family. This includes information on:
   - Ethnicity.
   - Disability.
   - Religion.
   - Child protection enquiries.
   - Child or young person's networks other than family networks.
   - Details of the involvement of other agencies, e.g. schools, health centres, GPs, other social services.
   - Details of action taken and reasons for action taken.

3. **Placement Information Record:** this is completed at the time the child or young person becomes looked after and must be given to all carers at the beginning of any placement as it contains the information you will need to provide the necessary care for a child placed with you. This document contains the following:
   - The parental agreement for the child to be looked after (where there is no court order on the child or young person).
   - Consent to specific medical treatment.
   - The delegation of responsibilities for the child or young person, including consent for the child to have overnight stays.
   - Details of contact arrangements.

4. **Chronology:** this document collects all the significant events, changes and movements in a child or young person's life. It helps to highlight patterns by pin pointing events and the significance of these events for a child. The chronology specifically collects information about the following:
   - A record of involvement with the social services.
   - A record of involvement in any child protection issues.
   - Health history.
   - Education, training and employment history.
   - A record of changes in the child/young person's legal status.
   - The placement history of a looked after child.
   - A record of any offences or criminal activity.
   - Details of significant events in the child's family/network.

5. **Closure Record:** this is used when a decision has been made to stop working with the child and their family. It records a summary of actions and services provided and the reasons for the decision to close the case.

Assessment documents

There are six documents designed to enable information to be gathered about the child and their family from a range of sources. They bring together information from all the agencies involved with the child or young person and their family and provide a focus for the combined information so there is a clear understanding about what is happening at any one time. From this, decisions can be made about what the needs are and what actions to take.

1. **Initial Assessment Record:** this records the initial assessment on the child or young person and their family. It establishes if a child is in need and what services and actions are necessary to respond to these needs. It will also identify if a Core Assessment is necessary or may lead to a strategy discussion or meeting if there is suspicion that a child is being harmed or likely to be harmed or abused (see Chapter 20 *Child Protection*).

2. **Core Assessment Record:** this is used when a detailed and in-depth assessment is necessary, particularly when a child's circumstances are complex. There are six age-related core assessments records:
   - Pre-birth-12 months
   - Age 1-2
   - Age 3-4
   - Age 5-10
   - Age 11-15
   - Age 16 and over

   The Core Assessment Record is used to develop the Child's Plan and continues the process of collecting information necessary to enable the monitoring of the child or young person's progress. Where a child or young person is to remain looked after, further assessments will be recorded using the Assessment and Progress Records.

3. **Record of Strategy Discussion:** this is used when there is suspicion that a child is being harmed or abused or likely to be harmed and where the decisions of a strategy discussion or meeting are recorded.

4. **Record of Outcome of s47enquiries:** s47 enquiries are the enquiries that social services must make to investigate suspicions of child abuse. This document records the outcome of the enquiries/investigations and the outcome of the Core Assessment which will be taking place at the same time and records details of the further action necessary.

5. **Initial Child Protection Conference Report:** this document contains a summary of the information gathered by social services in preparation for the initial child protection conference. It will also contain the decisions made by those at the conference including if the child's name is to be placed on the child protection register (see Chapter 20 *Child Protection*).

6. The Assessment and Progress Record: there are four age-related Assessment and Progress Records:
   - Age 1-2
   - Age 3-4
   - Age 5-10
   - Age 11-15

These documents are designed to enable a detailed history of the child's achievements, development, interests and abilities to be recorded. They set out a number of age-related milestones, developments or skills that a parent would be expected to promote for their child and enable these important aspects to be recorded and saved for the child in a way that has meaning for them and is informative.

These very detailed documents concentrate on seven areas. These areas are normally called dimensions:

- health
- education
- identity
- family and social relationships
- social presentation
- emotional and behavioural development
- self care skills

Foster carers will be expected to help complete and update these records regularly and will be required to start this task from the second review (i.e. four months from the start of the placement) and for it to have been completed by the time of the child's third review, (i.e., when the child has been with you for 10 months).

Planning documents

The documents used for planning for a child who is looked after include documents with various functions and are described above. The Integrated Children's System is designed to create 'joined up' documentation:

1. **Initial Assessment Record, the Record of Outcome of s47 enquiries and Initial Child Protection Conference Report:** after these documents have been used, plans must be drawn up that address the immediate or short-term needs that have been identified and these must be included in the overall planning for the child or young person.

2. **Child/Young Person's Care Plan:** this is completed following a Core Assessment. It is also the Child Protection Plan for any child or young person whose name has been on the child protection register. The Child/Young Person's Plan will still be necessary for a child whose name has been removed from the child protection register or who is no longer being looked after but who still remains a child/young person in need of advice or support from social services.

    The Care Plan is in two parts: Part one sets out the overall plan which can only be changed at a child/young person looked after review. Part two lists what services are necessary to meet the child/young person's needs. The Care Plan includes the Personal Education Plan (PEP) (see Chapter 23 *Education*), health plan and the plan for permanence. This is also the main document required by the Family Court if the child or young person is the subject of legal proceedings.

3. **Adoption Plan:** this is completed when there has been a clear decision that the child should be adopted. The adoption plan should contain details of the process and timescales involved.

4. **Pathway Plan:** Pathway Plans will be required for most children as a preparation for leaving care and preparing for adult life (see Chapter 24 *Leaving Care*). This plan is used to assess the needs at this specific time in a young person's life and is divided into two parts. Part one records the assessed needs and part two identifies the services which will support the young person as they progress into adult life. Where a young person has a Pathway Plan, this will replace part two of the Child/Young Person's Care Plan.

Review document

The Child/Young Person's Review: this is the document that is used at all the reviews undertaken on a child who is looked after. It is used to review the Child/Young Person's Care Plan, the Child Protection Plan and the Pathway Plan.

What does this mean for you?

As a carer, you play a major role in the process of caring for looked after children. Here are some points to remember:

- Along with your supervising social worker, you need to ensure that at the time of a placement, those bringing the child or young person will have with them the vital information you will need on the child, specifically the Placement Information Record, but you will also need other documents such as the Care Plan.
- You will need to be available for a placement meeting which needs to consider what you are required to do for the child or young person and what others are to do.
- There will be regular reviews, normally held at the place the child lives, although in a few instances, it may be held at other venues.
- The child's first review should take place within a month of the start of the placement, then within the next three months, and thereafter at no less than six months intervals.

These time spans are maximum time periods and you may be asked to attend a review more frequently especially if plans are rapidly changing for that young person. The review is the plan-making meeting for the young person and if plans change, they should be done so within these meetings.

Supplementary documents kept on the child or young person

You should be aware that there are other documents which may be kept on the child/young person which you may need to have a copy of:

- Information on the child/young person's educational needs, i.e. copy of the educational statement, if the child needs extra support at school or has special needs.
- Court orders on the child, child's birth certificate if appropriate.
- Psychiatric reports.

The Assessment and Progress Records

The Assessment and Progress Records (APR) bring together the various aspects or skills that all parents should ensure their child is capable of. They record details that parents remember or do or teach their own child at particular ages. Most parents do not need to make detailed record of their child's history and progress because they are likely to remember them but those children who are looked after may not have any one particular carer who can do this for them throughout their lives. It is essential therefore that the local authority, as the corporate parent, makes sure this information is recorded for the child or young person and you will have a vital role in this.

The decision to start the Assessment and Progress Record and who will be responsible for the co-ordination will be discussed and taken at the review. Information contained on the Assessment and Progress Record will also be used at consequent reviews.

Children and young people should be encouraged to participate in the Assessment and Progress Record as much as possible or they can decide who they want to help them with it.

It is the responsibility of the social worker to co-ordinate the collation of the various information held by teachers, health workers, youth workers and others involved in the child/young person's life. However, as a carer, you may have a good or close relationship with some of these people so it may be appropriate, with the agreement of the social worker that you approach these people instead. The whole point is to collect as much useful information on the child or young person as possible.

The completion of the Assessment and Progress Records is crucial. They should be seen as important and vital work tools and not just an exercise in ticking boxes. You should plan to use them in advance and consider how and when you will approach the young person. They need to be done steadily. Some of the sections should be approached sensitively and your supervising social worker should be on hand to assist and guide you through the process.

Some young people may like to keep their own copy as it is being completed. If this is the case for the young person you are caring for, ask the social worker or your supervising social worker for an extra copy although you may be able to print out copies from your own computer.

Chapter 16

Keeping Records and Accessing Records

Record keeping

The carer is trained and provided with the necessary equipment to record significant life events for the child, and to encourage the child to make such recordings, including photograph albums.

NMS 24.7

NMS The National Minimum Standards also say the *fostering service* must ensure that:

- There is a clear policy about what information is kept on files held by the agency and local authorities that it explains the purpose, format and contents of these files (**NMS 24.2**).
- Foster carers know why a child is to be fostered and know what is expected from the placement, purpose of the placement, details of the young person's legal status and the proposed length of the placement (**NMS 24.4**).
- The foster carer works with the child to understand their past and to make sense of it. The foster carer keeps information and items to help the child remember (**NMS 24.5**) and the carer is provided with the necessary training and equipment to record significant aspects of the child's life and where possible, the carer encourages the child to keep their own records such as photos (**NMS 24.7**).
- Foster carers have all the necessary paperwork to help the child understand and come to terms with their past and access to all the necessary information to do this. If the fostering agency is unable to obtain the information from the local authority, then a copy of the letter of request is kept on file (**NMS 24.6**).
- The carer is clear about how they must store confidential information and are also clear about the information they are expected to keep and what information they are to return to the fostering service (**NMS 24.8**).
- There are 'permanent, private and secure' records kept on you at the agency office and the agency must have a policy that encourages you to see your records and where necessary to have an input into what is written about you via the agency's access to records policy (**NMS 25.6** and **25.12**). Your records should be kept in line with the agency's written policy on the retention of files (**NMS 25.7**).
- Information kept on you or by you should be recorded in an easily readable way, be non-stigmatising and make clear what is an opinion and what is information from a third party (**NMS 25.9**).

> **UKNS** The UK National Standards for Foster Care also include the following:
>
> - Individual case records are kept on each child and that this is kept separately from the family's and the foster carer's records (**UKNS 8.2**) and that the child, his parents and carers know that these records are kept and they are kept securely and that only authorised people can see them (**UKNS 8.3**).
> - Clear details are kept of the child's ethnic, religious, cultural and linguistic background as well as other information about the child's identity or any disability the child may have. That care plans or placement agreements contain all the details about the support needs and resources offered for the child as well as record progress (**UKNS 8.4**).
> - That all case records clearly indicate the views and wishes as expressed by the child and evidence of how these have been taken into account is clearly recorded (**UKNS 8.9**).

What does this mean for you?

There is a great recognition of the need for foster carers to keep records and notes of their fostering. This is not just when specifically called to do so, for instance, when you are to monitor an aspect of a child's behaviour or you need to compile information and evidence for court, but also, it is a vital aspect of safer caring. Real concerns about the increasing numbers of allegations against carers means that in some cases, your recordings could minimise the impact of an allegation made against you or may eliminate it.

Your agency should have its own policy about how to record, what to record and the frequency of it (**NMS 24.2**). Some of the information the policy should contain is produced below.

Most carers are issued with a diary and you may be in the habit of making regular notes in it. This is however, not advisable, as the diary is more of a public document which you will be using regularly to check, for example, on appointments or meetings. It is important that you keep separate notes that you can transfer into reports for your supervising social worker or the young person's social worker. This information is highly confidential and must not be left lying around but kept in a secure place or in your lockable file box (**NMS 25.4**). If you are in any doubt, you should discuss the storage of this information with your supervising social worker who should advise if you have taken adequate precautions.

It is advisable that you keep daily records that are dated and initialled. This is especially relevant if keeping records for court as you may be asked if your records are contemporaneous – i.e. if they were written immediately after the event. Dating and initialling or signing your record also gives some safeguard in case someone tries to tamper with the information. However, most of the records you keep will not be for court but are likely to be called upon if there is a complaint or a child protection investigation has been started.

Remember it is one of the rules of safer caring that you keep a good record of issues and share the information quickly and regularly with your supervising social worker and the young person's social worker. In this way you will have recorded and passed on information about specific events that may later be the subject of an investigation or enquiry. You will also be able to show what efforts and attempts you made to resolve or raise matters.

However, most of the recording will be ultimately to record events and issues for the child in your care to help them to make sense of their lives as well as to remember different incidents or events or even the sequence within which something occurred. It is important to keep the memory of childhood alive especially given the likely moves children in the care system will have. It is sad that the majority of children looked after will not have one significant adult who will be able to tell them for example, when they cut their first tooth or what happened on the first day of school.

Maintaining written recordings are not the only way that you should be keeping young people's memories. You should also be keeping photographs, keep sakes, drawings, letters etc. In fact, the type of mementos you would keep for your own child. Help young people to value this by also encouraging them (**NMS 24.5**). This type of recording is similar to when you may be called to prepare a life story for a child/young person. In recognition of the importance of this work and the skills necessary your agency should ensure you receive the necessary training (**NMS 24.7**).

Some guidance about recording

- Record the use of sanctions or punishments; this should be done as soon as possible during the day.
- Record the young person's absences from the foster home.
- Record fights, disputes and disagreements.
- Make recordings of the young person's contact (**NMS 10.9**).
- Note the contact and meetings you may have had with the young person's social worker (especially if decisions are made), their school, any health appointments and any other activities which should be recorded that relate to the health and welfare of the young person.
- Do summaries on the young person in time for their review so that you are able to fill in the consultation documents.
- If asked to complete an Action and Progress Record, work out a way of recording the necessary details to be able to complete it as effectively as possible.
- Encourage young people to keep their own records, especially their own Assessment and Progress Records and for their Looked After Reviews. Share appropriate information written about the young person with them (**NMS 25.12**).
- Keep all sensitive and confidential information safely locked up (**NMS 25.4**).
- Give copies of your recordings regularly to your supervising social worker and the young person's social worker.
- Make sure your entries if written by hand, are legible and as factual as possible. It is not always possible to be objective but it would be useful to indicate what your own emotions were when writing the entry (**NMS 25.9**).

- Make sure you indicate fact from speculation, hearsay and third party information (**NMS 25.9**)
- Keep mementos of the child (**NMS 24.5**).
- Make sure all your records are signed and dated.

Remember you can keep your own recordings but anything directly relating to the young person, i.e. all their Looked After Children forms should be returned to the local authority once the young person has moved from you (**NMS 25.5** and **25.7**). Your supervising social worker will be able to advise you more on this.

How long should I keep my records for?

Social services departments have to keep their records on all children they have looked after for 75 years. Speak to your supervising social worker about what you should or should not retain as your agency should have its own policy on the retention of files, records and information you have produced (**NMS 25.7**).

Access to records

All carers and children looked after can have access to their *own* records. Your agency should keep separate records for you and separate records for children looked after (**NMS 25.2**). When seeking access to records you will only be allowed to see information relating to you. All third party information will need to be removed although there should not be much of this information in your file. Various documents such as your personal references may also be removed from your file unless your referees gave permission for you to see them.

Should you wish to see your file you will need to write to your agency and they should arrange for you to see your file within a clearly specified period. Check what your agency's policy is on this. While you will not be allowed to remove any information from your records, you will be able to take copies and can make your comments about information stored.

Chapter 17

Confidentiality

Confidentiality

Confidential records are stored securely at all times and there is a clear policy on access.
NMS 25.4

Confidentiality is implicit in all functions of the fostering task.

What does this mean for you?

Not only is confidentiality a vital component of caring for a young person but it is also important that the young person clearly witnesses and understands the way you keep their confidence. Carers must always lock away sensitive information about the young person and only share information with those authorised to have it, and, at the end of placements, all information you hold on the child must be returned with the child to the local authority.

There are basic rules that you as carers will be familiar with and issues around confidentiality should be contained in your foster care agreement (see Chapter 8 *The Foster Care Agreement*).

A cover story

The way you share information with the rest of the family can help the child/young person construct a 'cover story' which will enable them and the rest of your family to respond to questions and situations without compromising the child or young person. Your supervising social worker will be able to help you with this but it will be important to work with the child/young person and establish what they are going to be comfortable with other people knowing about themselves and being in foster care.

Think in advance about how to prepare *your own* children and support network with the cover story so that a safe family culture is developed. Remember that the cover story should be based on reality but should be discrete enough to allow the young person not to feel exposed.

See also Chapter 16 *Keeping Records and Accessing Records*.

Chapter 18

Safety in the Home

Health and safety in the foster home

The fostering service makes available foster carers who provide a safe, healthy and nurturing environment.

NMS 6.1

NMS The National Minimum Standards also say the *fostering service* must ensure that:

- They have approved foster carers who can provide a safe, healthy and nurturing home environment for the child to live and enjoy family life (**NMS 6.2**).
- If a child has been abused or has abused another child, then the child's needs and the needs of all the other children in the household must be assessed before any agreement is made to allow the sharing of bedrooms. This assessment should be made in writing (**NMS 6.5**).
- That foster carers are given training, both during the preparation period and on a regular basis which covers all aspects of health and safety. Foster carers must also be given *written* guidelines on their responsibilities for health and safety (**NMS 6.7**).

Other standards are included in the rest of this chapter under specific headings.

UKNS The UK National Standards for Foster Care also include the following:

- Carers should help the child be aware of risks in the home, for instance from electrical equipment, fire or dangerous chemicals (**UKNS 6.5**) and where such materials/equipment need to be in the home that they are locked away, their use supervised or the access to children is prevented (**UKNS 6.4**).
- That the carer has a clear health and safety guidance for their home (**UKNS 6.7**).

What does this mean for you?

Health and safety has always been an important issue in fostering but not until the introduction of the UK National Standards and the National Minimum Standards has there been a national attempt at consistency and the setting of standards. These standards are now quite clear so that expectations on carers have become transparent. It is useful for you to check through this section from time to time. It is also important that you attend regular training on the various aspects of health and safety, as it is a developing field. Health and safety is also one of the areas your supervising social worker will be reviewing throughout the year and will be specifically commenting on for your annual foster care review (**NMS 6.2**). See your agency's health and safety check list which will include the following.:

Accommodation

- The home is warm, adequately furnished and decorated and is maintained to a good standard of cleanliness and hygiene (**NMS 6.3**).
- There must be sufficient space and facilities for play, doing homework and quiet space where a young person can be alone and have privacy. If the child or young person has a disability, then the space must be suitable for their needs (**NMS 6.4**).
- Many fostering agencies insist that all children or young people cared for have their own bedroom, which they may only share with their own siblings. A child may want to share with a child other than a sibling. This *should only be agreed* with the express agreement of the child's social worker and others who will be involved. However, if the child has a history of abuse or there is a risk that the child may abuse other children then an assessment of the needs of all the children in the household should be made before the sharing of rooms is allowed. The assessment must be recorded in writing (**NMS 6.5**).
- As the carer, one of your roles is to give guidance to children and young people on how they may keep themselves safe in the home and this should include an understanding of dangerous materials, electrical equipment and fire risks (**UKNSs – 6.5**).
- The home, gardens and its surroundings must be fitted with safety devices or barriers to ensure that there are no risks or hazards that may cause injury or harm, e.g. ponds must be made safe and fencing should be secure. Children and young people must be protected from any foreseeable hazards that there may be. (**NMS 6.6**).
- The home must also be fitted with the necessary devices such as fire alarm/smoke detectors, fire extinguishers, and fire blankets and should be kept in a readily accessible place (**NMS 6.6**).
- There must also be a fully stocked First Aid Box and all carers should be familiar with basic First Aid and basic responses to common accidents in the home. This will be covered in training offered to all carers and carers are expected to ensure that they keep up to date with developments.
- The handbook given to you by your agency is also a source of guidance (**NMS 6.7**).

Transportation

Where the foster carer is expected to provide transport for the child, the fostering service ensures this is safe and appropriate to the child's needs.

NMS 6.8

- Foster carers must ensure that all the vehicles they use to transport children/young people comply with all the safety advice and requirements. All cars *must* be roadworthy, taxed and insured. They should also be fitted with the required safety belts or properly fitted restraint for a young child or person with a disability. Carers should not exceed the number of passengers allowed – i.e., a normal family car would take two people in the front and three passengers in the back. Overloading a family car *may* lead to the invalidation of your insurance especially if an accident is caused by being distracted by passengers.

- Young children should not be seated in the front passenger seat. Get advice about this from the child's social worker or your supervising social worker.
- Safety helmets should always be worn if using bikes or motor bikes and outer garments should always have florescent strips to ensure visibility. All bikes and motor bikes should be road worthy and the lights, reflectors, alarms and horns should also be regularly checked.
- As part of the yearly health and safety check you will be expected to produce your vehicle documents and these will be confirmed within the health and safety check which should be undertaken for your annual review.

Home safety

All children and young people are different and will need different safety boundaries and practices. You need to ensure that you practice the highest level of safety possible and have a good understanding of the needs of each and every different child you may care for. Below is a list of other considerations, which are not definitive but that you should be aware of. When in doubt, discuss these with your supervising social worker:

- Alcohol, drugs, other intoxicating substances, dangerous liquids and chemicals should be out of reach or locked away.
- There should be no pornographic material on the premises and books, videos, CDs etc. that are considered educational but contain information of a sexual nature should have their use supervised.
- Money and valuables should be locked out of reach but in any event, large sums should not generally be kept in the home.
- Use of the internet should be supervised or screened, as should the watching of some programmes on television.
- All medicines should be locked and out of the way. The use of medicines should be supervised.
- There should be no guns or weapons on the premises.
- All electrical appliances and fittings must be sound and regularly checked.
- Safety glass must be installed in the appropriate areas and stickers used to ensure that the glass is visible.
- All windows should be appropriately secured to prevent young people from falling out, but must also open up sufficiently as an escape route in case of fire.
- The stairs, banisters and any carpet covering should be secure.
- Food should be stored and refrigerated as recommended by the manufacturer.
- There should not be any portable gas or paraffin heaters.
- Household heating should be safe, appropriately calibrated and adequate to heat the house and be serviced regularly.
- All gas appliances should be regularly serviced especially gas fires and gas boilers.
- The hot water supply should be appropriately calibrated or easily and safely useable for young people.
- Smoking areas should be clearly designated. The issue of smoking should be clearly agreed with the young person, their social worker and your supervising social worker. There must be an agreement that will safeguard the health, welfare and safety of the whole household.

The child or young person's general health and welfare

(See Chapter 21 *Health*.)

The UK National Standards for Foster Care underline the following responsibilities that carers have:

- That the child/young person you care for has enough clothing for their needs and that the clothes are in good condition (**UKNS 6.8**).
- That the child/young person is provided with a diet that meets their growing needs, their religious or cultural needs and takes into account what they enjoy eating (**UKNS 6.10**).
- That the child/young person is in an environment which is supportive and encouraging of the child to grow and thrive and where their emotional and developmental needs are addressed (**UKNS 6.11**).
- The child/young person is in an environment where their racial, ethnic, cultural, religious and sexual identity is nurtured and they are helped to value and enhance this (**UKNS 6.12**).
- The child is in an environment which stimulates and develops the child's play and learning. Where toys suitable for the child's age, interests and needs are provided which avoid for example racist or sexist stereotypes (**UKNS 6.13**).
- The foster family helps the child to maintain their positive relationships and interests and are encouraged to develop new ones (**UKNS 6.14**).

Managing some risks

As indicated above, the list is not definitive and it is possible that you may not be able to fulfil some of the considerations or that they may not be relevant. In all circumstances, speak to your supervising social worker who will also be able to assist in clarifying what becomes relevant and what does not. Remember, while it is imperative to prevent the preventable, it is also important that young people live within the confines of what is considered to be family life. You may be able to be less cautious with some children but not with others. Young people need to learn to live with acceptable risks, such as having access to painkillers when they have a headache. However if they are not capable of living with that 'risk' or you have doubts, lock them away as suggested. Inform your supervising social worker of any adjustments you may be making to the list above, especially if you are working with a young person towards independence. The responsibility for managing risks in these circumstances will then be a shared one between you and the agency (and also the child's social worker) and these should be aspects that are contained in your safer caring document.

Reporting accidents or incidents

It is vital that you keep accurate and detailed records of any accidents or incidents involving the children you are caring for. Ensure, in all circumstances that once you have addressed the child's needs, you report it as soon as possible afterwards to the child's social worker and to your agency.

Record the incident. You don't necessarily need to write a great deal but you need to record the time, date, nature of the accident or incident and your actions and what happened. (See Chapter 16 *Keeping Records and Accessing Records*.)

Pets and animals

Animals that are commonly kept as pets normally present an acceptable risk within a foster home provided adequate hygiene, supervision and that they are kept away from some of the areas in the home. If you are considering having a pet that would not be considered a common household pet, speak to your supervising social worker first.

All dogs and cats should be fully vaccinated, wormed and de-fleaed as necessary or as recommended by a vet. They must also be fully in your control and not prone to jumping up at young people/strangers without being provoked. It is important to consider that young people who may come to stay with you may be frightened of animals. Equally, animals can be extremely comforting to children.

The keeping of dangerous breeds of dogs included in the Dangerous Dogs Act 1991 should not be accepted in any foster homes. These are Pit Bull Terrier, Japanese Towser, Dogo Argentino and Fila Braziliero. In addition, it should be noted that the following breeds are also considered to pose a threat to health and safety and you should seek advice from your supervising social worker before considering them as pets. They are Rottweiller, Alsatian (German Shepherd), Doberman or Bandog.

You may be asked by the agency to provide proof that your dog is under your control and the RSPCA or your vet will be able to do a risk assessment.

Chapter 19

Safer Caring

Safer Caring

Safe caring guidelines are provided, based on a written policy, for each foster home, in consultation with the carer and everyone else in the household. The guidelines are cleared with the child's social worker and are explained clearly and appropriately to the child.

NMS 9.3

NMS The National Minimum standards say the *fostering service* must ensure that:

- The training provided to you includes:
  - caring for a child who has been abused
  - safe(r) caring skills
  - managing behaviour
  - recognising signs of abuse
  - ways of boosting and maintaining a child's self-esteem (**NMS 9.2**)
- You are able to develop safe(r) caring guidelines for your home which are developed with, where possible:
  - everyone in your household including your own children
  - your support network, if they are actively involved with the child
  - the child's social worker
  - the foster child (**NMS 11** and **NMS 9.7**)
  - and where possible, the foster child's family (**NMS 9.3**)
- You get all the information available on a fostered child and their family to enable you to protect:
  - the foster child
  - your own children and any others you may be responsible for as well as
  - you and your partner
  - your support network (**NMS 9.7**)
- Clear written guidance on acceptable forms of restraining a child is given, and make it clear to you that no form of corporal punishment is acceptable (**NMS 9.4**).
- Clear guidance and information is given on how children may be susceptible to bullying. The agency must also have policies and procedures in place to help you recognise, record and address instances of bullying that you may have to cope with (**NMS 9.6**).
- Clear written procedures are given for you to use if the foster child goes missing (**NMS 9.8**).

→

- All agencies will need to keep details and statistics on how they run the service and specifically about the lives of the children they are caring for. They will therefore be keeping details of allegations or complaints against the foster carer and the conclusions to these (**NMS 9.5**).

UKNS The UK National Standards for Foster Care also include the following:

- A responsibility on the child's social worker to ensure that the foster child is taught self care and self protection skills (**UKNS 7.4**).
- Reminds carers that all adults living in a foster home or who will be with the child for significant times on their own must be subject to all necessary checks (**UKNS 7.5**).

Safer caring as well as the wider subject of child protection and abuse will be part of the on-going training offered by your agency in line with **NMS 9.2**. The Fostering Network's *Safer Caring* is an invaluable guide to all those within the fostering and child care field and gives clear messages on how to uphold the safety of young people, your family and you as carers. It is based on the principle that prevention is better than cure.

What does this mean for you?

- Ensure that you have all the available information on the young person so that you may be able to protect the young person, your own children and other children you may be responsible for and yourselves (**NMS 9.7**). Get this in advance of the placement.
- Consider carefully and discuss with your supervising social worker and the rest of your family whether the child would fit into your home and your family lifestyle. Again, get as much information on the child; meet with the child, their family or previous carers.
- Ensure that all the documents relating to the young person are shared with you as soon as possible. Very few children who come into the care system are completely unknown.
- Ensure that you have your supervising social worker with you during meetings to support you.
- Ensure you know what support is on offer to you, your family and the young person and that it includes access to a 24 hour help line service if possible. Where agencies do not have a dedicated 24 hour help line they will have an out of hours service which is equipped to deal with emergencies that arise outside normal office hours.
- Ensure you are provided with the training listed earlier in this section.
- Ensure that you understand and are able to comply with the fact that under no circumstance must you use any form of corporal punishment (**NMS 9.4**). (Details of behaviour management techniques are set out in Chapter 25 *Managing Behaviour*.)
- Ensure you understand and are familiar with your agency's anti-bullying policy (**NMS 9.6**) (guidance on this is contained in Chapter 27 *Bullying*).
- Ensure you understand and are familiar with your agency's guidance on what to do if a child is missing from home as detailed in Chapter 26 *When a Child is Missing From Home*.

These measures are all aimed at equipping and empowering you to take reasonable steps to protect you and those around you. Your supervising social worker will also advise on issues such as household and car safety and this will be reviewed at least annually (see Chapter 18 *Safety in the Home*).

Other things to remember about safer caring

- Make sure you report and record incidents, accidents and emergencies.
- Make your house rules and safer caring document clear to the young person, your own children and check them out with the child's social worker and your supervising worker (**NMS 9.3**). Make sure that the child or young person understands them. You may have to think of inventive ways to get the message across or you may just have to be persistent!
- Only leave children with people who are authorised to care for them, i.e. who are part of a named support network and who have had the necessary checks done.
- Have clear rules about privacy, including in bedrooms and bathrooms.
- Have clear rules about touching and what is good and bad touching.
- Avoid tickling and wrestling games.
- Young people should not be sharing bedrooms if there is a risk of them abusing other children or if they themselves have been abused.
- There should be clear rules on how people dress in the house.
- Young people should always have access to food and drink or extra food and drink (but not alcohol). Withholding food should not be used as a punishment.
- Dangerous and addictive substances should be locked and out of reach.
- There should be clear return times from school or from an evening out which everyone should know and keep to.
- The use of computer games and access to the internet or the television should be supervised or locks put in place.

This list not exhaustive. You and your supervising social worker will be able to discuss the information you have on each child and devise routines and rules that should help you to care for children safely. This is the kind of information your household safe(r) guidance should contain.

Remember, under no circumstances must a foster carer use corporal punishment (**NMS 9.4**). See Chapter 25 *Managing a Child's Behaviour*.

Chapter 20

Child Protection

Child protection

The fostering service protects each child or young person from all forms of abuse, neglect, exploitation and deprivation.

NMS 9.1

> **NMS** The National Minimum Standards also say the *fostering service* must ensure that:
>
> - That all carers are clear that they must not administer corporal punishment (**NMS 9.4**).
> - They have systems to collect the information, details, numbers etc of all allegations of neglect or abuse of a child in foster care and that this information is reviewed so that further cases can be prevented (**NMS 9.5**).

> **UKNS** The UK National Standards for Foster Care also include the following:
>
> - That all training for foster carers includes training on children who have been abused and how to recognise the signs (**UKNS 7.1**).
> - That all children are taught self protection skills (**UKNS 7.4**).
> - That there are clear procedures for dealing with allegations of abuse or neglect in foster care (**UKNS 7.6**).
> - That the local authority in consultation with the child, pursues compensation for any child who has been abused in foster care, or who was abused prior to a placement in foster care (**UKNS 7.8**).

Child protection is a very difficult and stressful thing to have to deal with and vigilance and safer caring are necessary to prevent or at least alleviate situations. The following is an attempt to show what your role and the roles of others would be within the child protection process.

Your role when a child or young person tells you that they have been abused

The child or young person you are caring for may have been hurt or spoken about abuse that may have happened recently or some time ago. Either way, they are likely to be very distressed and worried about what is going to happen to them. Your role is to support the young person and in doing so, you need to make them feel confident that they have done the right thing and understand why you have to inform their social worker. This may be the first time that they have ever confided in somebody or perhaps, sadly, they have told someone in their past and nothing was seemingly done. You must listen and be supportive and although you should not specifically ask questions of the young person about the incident, you must *listen*, *record* and *reassure*. Accurate recording is vital. *You must inform the child's social worker and your supervising social worker.*

Be clear with the child that even if they consider what they are telling you to be a secret, that there are some secrets that must be shared but that you and the authorities will do all they can to make the child as comfortable about painful matters as is possible to do.

You should have a copy of the child protection procedures and you need to be familiar with them so you will know how to respond and support a young person through all the stages of the investigation/process. Safeguarding children is one of the core training courses organised by your agency and it is imperative that all those involved in the fostering task undergo regular training on this. Each carer needs to be aware of the procedures because allegations and disclosures may arise at any time. You should also explain child protection to your own children as a young person is just as likely to tell one of your children as they are to you.

Allegations of abuse can be made against you, your partner, your children or indeed anyone that the young person has access to. Sometimes they may be malicious but equally they may not be because unfortunately, carers or members of a carer's family or network have abused children. Where at all possible, you must be vigilant (see Chapter 19 *Safer Caring*). Not only should you be fostering in a safe way but you need *to be seen* to be doing it. Also see Chapter 15 *Looked After Documents* for more information on the documents used during child protection investigations and what information is collected and recorded.

Fostering agencies should ensure that foster carers have access to the following:

- The child protection procedures for the local authority in which they live.
- The child protection procedures for the agency if different from above.
- Leaflets and articles; The Fostering Network and the British Agencies for Adoption and Fostering (BAAF) have invaluable and readable information on for example fostering a child who has been sexually abused, child abuse and accusations against foster carers.
- Safe Caring document for the foster home.
- Legal cover; to cover you and your network against court proceedings – see Chapter 9 *Terms and Conditions for Foster Carers*.
- Support from the agency throughout the process; this will follow different routes especially if you or one of your household is accused of abusing a child but this will be made clear to you in writing should this be the case (see Chapter 28 *Children Making Complaints*).

The principles of child protection

- Each authority has a legal duty to protect children and young people.
- All investigations of alleged abuse must be pursued rigorously but with an open mind and a balanced approach.

- No allegation can be ignored.
- The allegation is investigated within the time limits that each authority has set itself.
- The young person must be supported throughout the process.
- Once an allegation is made it must be investigated thoroughly, no matter who is involved.
- In every investigation the local authority's child protection procedures will be followed at all times. This usually means that all independent fostering agencies will co-operate with whatever the relevant local authority's procedures are for that young person.

Your role in the child protection process

When a young person makes a disclosure you should record the information and reassure the young person. You must also as soon as is possible, inform your supervising social worker and the young person's social worker or their manager. This must be on the day. Tell the child or young person what you will do and keep them informed.

If the disclosure is made outside office hours you should seek advice from the 24-hour help line which will be able to advise further. In general, if the young person is safe, not in distress and does not need medical treatment/investigation, then it can probably wait until the next working day. You should try to calm the young person and encourage them to try and sleep.

It is essential that you follow the child protection procedure in the event of a child speaking about abuse or if you think a child may have been abused.

It will be the role of the local authority in which you live to take the lead on the task of investigating what has happened.

If you are caring for a child with a disability it is important to remember that they can be more vulnerable to abuse for a number of reasons. For example, they may not be able to defend themselves or shout, they may have daily experiences of intimate physical care and they may have limited knowledge of sex and sexuality.

Allegations made against carers or a member of their family: this will be covered in Chapter 28 *Children Making Complaints*.

The child protection register

Once the initial child protection conference has taken place a decision needs to be recorded as to whether a child or young person's name is to be placed on the child protection register. Reasons for the decision will be recorded on the Initial Child Protection Conference Report and this will clearly set out what and who the child is to be protected from (see also Chapter 15 *Looked After Children Documents*).

What are the definitions of child abuse?

Child abuse is commonly defined in five different ways and they are indicated below. A list of some signs or symptoms to look out for are outlined, but they should not be considered on their own. They act as a guide as to what to consider within the *whole* picture of what the young person is presenting or saying.

Definition of sexual abuse:
> The actual or likely sexual exploitation of a child or adolescent.

Physical warning signs:
- Genital injuries, infections, soreness, itching, pain.
- Soiling or retention.
- Pregnancy.
- Sexually transmitted diseases.
- Age inappropriate sexual knowledge or behaviour.

Behavioural and emotional warning signs:
- Impeccable behaviour.
- Behaviour with sexual overtones.
- Frequent or explicit sexual preoccupation in talk and play.
- Sexually provocative with adults.
- Hinting at sexual activity or secrets through words, play or drawings.
- Sexual activity between young people.
- Withdrawn, fearful aggressive behaviour to peers or adults.
- Absconding.
- Suicide or self harm.
- Psychiatric problems.
- Severe sleep disturbance.
- Inappropriate displays of affection between child and adult.
- Poor concentration.
- Reluctance to participate in physical games/activities.

Definition of physical abuse:
> The actual or likely physical injury to a child, or failure to prevent physical injury (or suffering) to a child including deliberate poisoning, suffocation and Munchausen Syndrome by Proxy*.

*Munchausen Syndrome by Proxy is where a carer deliberately harms a child to gain attention for themselves as a good and vigilant carer.

Warning signs:
- non-accidental injuries (could lead to death)
- fractures
- burns and scalds
- internal injuries
- bruises
- cigarette burns
- bites
- scarring

Burns and scalds:
- Uniform depth over large area is suspicious.
- Scalds/burns with clear outlines are suspicious i.e., that look like socks around a child's

foot (conducive to the child's foot being pushed down into hot water) – likewise on the child's bottom – the child being forced to sit in hot water. Ordinarily if the child accidentally tries to get into a hot bath they will have splash marks.
- Small round burns which dip in the middle could be caused by cigarettes.
- Friction burns on bony areas.

Scars and fractures:
- Numerous number of scars of different ages.
- Scars of an unusual shape.
- Fractures or scars which seem to have healed by themselves.
- Pain, swelling, discolouration over limb or joint.
- Fractures for a child under one year old or very immature baby.

It is extremely uncommon for the areas indicated below to become bruised accidentally:
- Backs of legs and buttocks.
- Mouth, cheeks, behind the ears.
- Stomach and chest.
- Under arm.
- Genital and rectal area.
- Neck.

Definition of emotional abuse:
Emotional abuse may take the form of failing to meet the child's need for affection, attention and stimulation (even though good physical care may be provided). It may also be constant verbal abuse, rejection, scapegoating, and threats of violence or attempts to frighten the child.

Conversely, some parents may be so over-protective and possessive that they prevent normal social contact or normal physical activity. Both these can be difficult to evidence but may have significant long-term effects on the child's development and ability to socialise.

Warning signs:
- Clingy and attention seeking.
- Low self-esteem.
- Apathy.
- Fearful or withdrawn.
- Seeking to please.
- Over familiar with many people especially strangers, constantly wishing to relate to people.

Definition of neglect:
Neglect includes not only poor physical care and inattention to the child's basic needs e.g. for regular feeding, cleanliness and clothing but also a failure to provide the necessary stimulation to sustain behaviour and emotional development.

Warning signs:
- Poor growth and no medical cause (dramatically improves away from home and once given a normal diet).
- Child dirty, unkempt and smelly.
- Lack of social responsiveness/ability to engage.
- Developmental delay.
- Self stimulating behaviour e.g. head banging, rocking.
- Numerous number of injuries which could have been prevented.
- Medical needs of child unmet causing chronic and severe nappy rash, missed immunisations, illness etc.

Definition of organised abuse:
The systematic sexual or physical abuse of children involving numbers of children and one perpetrator or numbers of children and several perpetrators. A feature of this type of abuse is that it can be highly organised and planned.

Chapter 21

Children's Health

Health

The fostering service ensures that it provides foster care services which help each child or young person in foster care to receive health care which meets her/his needs for physical, emotional and social development, together with information and training appropriate to her/his age and understanding to enable informed participation in decisions about her/his health needs.

NMS 12.1

NMS The National Minimum Standards also say the *fostering service* must ensure that:

- The providers of fostering services are well informed and aware of the health services in their area and, in the area their foster carers live, including specialist health provisions and this information should be used when considering particular carers for a particular child. They must ensure that all the child's health needs can be continued and promoted within the foster placement (**NMS 12.2**) and must help the foster carer to access these services when it is necessary (**NMS 12.7**).
- Prior to a placement:
  - the carer is given full details of the child's health needs
  - the carer has a clear understanding of how to get consent to medical treatment for the child
  - if the necessary health details are not available before a placement then this must be obtained as a matter of urgency and a *high priority* must be given to ensuring this information is passed on to the carer (**NMS 12.3**).
- Carers are given full health records for the child they are caring for and that these records are up-dated regularly and where possible, shared with the child to help them understand their health needs. These records should go with the child when the child moves (**NMS 12.4**).
- Carers have specific training in the areas of:
  - general aspects of health
  - hygiene
  - first aid
  - health promotion
  - identifying infectious diseases (**NMS 12.5**).

→

- Carers are clear about their role in promoting the health needs of the children they care for specifically by:
  - registering a child with a doctor and dentist
  - taking children for health appointments, including with dentists and opticians
  - being aware of other health needs the child may have and helping them access these services and resources, and being an advocate for them
  - promoting a healthy lifestyle for the child by including a healthy diet, personal hygiene and generally promoting health issues (**NMS 12.6**).
- Carers are clear about their role in actively providing information about the child's health and health needs particularly at the child's Looked After Children Reviews and also in the wider field of planning for the child (**NMS 12.8**).

UKNS The UK National Standards for Foster Care also include the following:

- That a full health assessment is carried out for each child in foster care at least once a year; this includes a physical examination. If the child does not agree to a physical examination then the authority must record what alternative actions and arrangements were made (**UKNS 10.1**). The child's informed consent to all health treatment must be actively sought and recorded (**UKNS 10.5**).
- The promotion of the health needs of the child should include therapy, counselling and sexual health (**UKNS 10.3**).
- All children should be involved and actively participate in the process of their own health needs as they are able and that the health care and advice offered to the child 'incorporates confidentiality and choice' (**UKNS 10.4**).
- All children, according to their ability to understand, are given clear details about their health history and informed of any significant medical problems in their birth family (**UKNS 10.6**).
- There must be a comprehensive understanding of the health of the child and it must be recorded where health needs are not met (**UKNS 10.7**).
- The improvements in the health and health education of children looked after is part of the foster agency's and local authority's plans for children (**UKNS 10.8**).
- Health authorities and health boards should provide services specifically needed to support the health needs of children looked after (**UKNS 10.9**) and that each health authority/health board designates a medical adviser for children who are looked after and that they have sufficient time allocated for this task (**UKNS 10.10**).

National Healthy Care Standards (NHCS)

The Department of Health issued the NHCS in 2002 as part of its *Guidance on Promoting the Health of Looked After Children*. The NHCS pull together all current initiatives and services under the government established Health Development Agency and are working on policies with the participation of young people, carers as well as other professionals.

Four key public health areas are being targeted for all NHCS partnerships. These include how they propose to address:

Health inequalities
- Reduction in rate of teenage pregnancies.
- Reduction in the number of people who smoke.
- To improve access to preventative and care services.

Mental health
- Improvements in mental and social well-being of children looked after (including access to sports, leisure and arts facilities).
- Improvements to the Child and Adolescent Mental Health Services (including mental health promotion and early intervention services).

Drugs
- Reduction in the use of illicit drugs.
- Reduction in the number of drug related deaths.
- Improvements in the access to drug treatment services.

Education
- Improvements in the educational attainment of children in care.

For further information on the NHCS see the Department for Education and Skills website.

What does this mean for you?

All carers should safeguard and promote the health of the young people they care for. This includes their physical and emotional well-being. The carer should ensure that the young person is able to develop good life style habits that will benefit them into independence and beyond. Children who are looked after are more likely to suffer from sickness and ill health so it is vital that your expectation for the young person is that they receive the best standard of health care available to them.

The Assessment and Progress Record is a good tool to use for charting the health of a young person and young people should be encouraged to use the tools themselves. They help the young person see what children should be doing, or should know, to promote their own health and also give guidance as to what a good parent should be providing for children's health needs.

All the young people you care for should have arrived with their Placement Information Record. These contain consent either from the young person's parent or if the child is under a Care Order, someone from the local authority giving consent for you to seek routine medical treatment for the young person (**NMS 12.3**). (See below for more information about consent.) They should also contain information on the young person's immediate health needs.

These documents should contain information about the young person's medical history and any conditions they may have and treatment they may be undergoing. It is essential that you have this information at the beginning of the placement as the child may have for instance, asthma, diabetes or allergies which would need to be monitored closely and immediately (**NMS 12.4**).

Where possible and practical, it would be much better for the child to remain with their own GP, dentist and optician. If this is not possible, ensure that the young person is registered with your GP as a matter of priority because the young person may be in urgent need of a statutory medical. Wherever possible, the *statutory* medical should take place with the young person's existing GP as they will have the medical records and they are likely to know the young person. Do not forget the child's dental and optical needs (**NMS 12.6**). It may not always be easy to get the children you care for registered with your own GP or dental practice but if you are having difficulties speak to your supervising social worker who should be able to help.

The health of the child also includes healthy eating and a balanced diet. You will need to spend some time getting to know what foods the young person likes or dislikes. Many young people may not have had the opportunity to experience a regular or balanced diet and it is important to establish a healthy eating routine in their lives. You should ensure that the young person has breakfast, lunch and dinner (**NMS 12.6**).

It is important to have food that the young person can have access to, cook or prepare for themselves. Adolescents, especially, are going to go through growing periods where they will consume a great deal although you should check and respond to the possibility that they may be eating for comfort or other reasons. Food should never be locked up and out the way or used as a sanction.

A young person could have special dietary needs either for medical or religious reasons. Ensure that you have been given the full facts and advice regarding this.

You will need to be familiar and informed about the health services in your area, including any specialist services (**NMS 12.2** and **12.7**). You should have discussed and researched some of these resources when going through your assessment to become a carer and this will be on your foster care profile as these details will also be considered when making a placement match especially with you. In fact, you should *not* have a placement made with you where it is not possible for the child to continue to obtain the health care they have been receiving or will need to receive.

Record all the relevant aspects of the young person's health so that proper planning can be undertaken for them (**NMS 12.8**).

Helping a young person to understand the importance of personal hygiene, about their body and physical development or their sexuality should also not be overlooked. It is likely that some young people will not have had the right person to ask the kind of inquisitive questions children want answering as they are growing and discovering the differences in themselves and in the opposite sex. Or perhaps they are full of half answered questions, presumptions and half truths. This is particularly difficult when discussing with a young person who may be embarrassed, shy or feels they may lose face when told of things they feel they know about already or should know about. Either way, these issues should be approached or it might be useful to talk to the person whom you think knows the young person best or with whom they are comfortable. It can then be agreed who is the right person to take on the task.

Dental care

Children who are looked after are particularly at risk from poor dental health as there have been connections made between tooth decay and social deprivation. Children may have come from chronically disrupted lifestyles where such care was not given importance or followed. The diet they had may also not have promoted healthy teeth.

Unlike medical care, it is not necessary for the child to remain with the same dentist unless they are in the middle of complicated dental treatment. A dentist would usually be able to decide on future treatment from an examination of a child's teeth.

A young person, particularly one who has not had regular dental checks should usually be seen by a dentist every 4-6 months throughout childhood.

Eye care

It is difficult to test the vision of a very young child but where there are concerns, i.e. squint or the 'eye looks wrong', your doctor, health visitor or a school nurse will be able to advise or refer to an eye clinic. Most high street opticians however are able to check the vision of school age children.

The many aspects of promoting the child and young person's health needs will be the themes of training throughout your fostering career and it is a requirement of the fostering task that both you and your partner attend.

The wishes and feelings of children and consent

Wherever possible, medical consent must be obtained from the child's parents. This will not be possible/necessary if:

- The child is on a Care Order.
- The child has been abandoned.
- The child's parents are not capable of giving consent, this could be because they have been deemed mentally incapable.
- The child's parents have signed over their authority/given permission to another (via the courts).

The wishes and feelings of the child should also be known using communication methods meaningful to the child. For children with limited communication skills, this means that suitable methods of communication should be sought.

Sexual health/sex education

Young people should be given constructive sex education and information in order to make good choices for themselves. Many young people will be sexually active at a young age and it is important that they can protect themselves. They may also be in turmoil and confusion about their sexuality or it may be the cause of bullying for them. You should not only give the young person information but should also incorporate the emotional aspects of relationships and self worth. A young person should be helped to build self-esteem so that peer pressure is minimised and they are able to make the right choices. Young people with disabilities may need more support in this area and may be more vulnerable to abusive relationships.

It is useful to cultivate good relationships with your GP or other health specialists.

Most young people in your care will be struggling to identify their sexual identity and this is a very demanding and confusing time for most young people but especially those looked after.

Some young people will not be able to deal with their new sexual drive and will need guidance and advice, for instance that it is OK to masturbate but that it must be done in private. Many young people are also likely to be emotionally confused and this can give off signals that could be misinterpreted (see Chapter 19 *Safer Caring*).

However, equally, carers should not allow children they are looking after to get involved in activities that a good parent would prevent. You will have the same moral and legal duties towards all children in your care and therefore you must report if you suspect that a young person is being sexually abused or is instigating it. Remember that it is an offence to have sexual relations with a child who is under the age of consent.

These issues are also traditionally difficult for young people to talk about so it is imperative that you feel sufficiently comfortable to enable them to feel as relaxed as possible. Young people who are looked after are more likely to have unwanted pregnancies or be young parents than other young people. They are also more likely to be drawn into prostitution or come into contact with sexually transmitted diseases. Some young people who may have been abused themselves may be perpetrators of sexual abuse on other children and young people. The issues are complex and therefore, openness from the carer about all related issues is necessary. Of course it is not possible to answer all a young person's questions but you should know how to contact; health clinics, gay and lesbian help lines, Brook Advisory and agencies dealing with sexually transmitted diseases for instance. Keeping literature on these subjects in a place that is not public but where the young person would have access to them when they need them would be useful and still give the young person privacy. There is also very good information on computers or CDs.

If the young person is sexually active and over 16 years of age

Be open and available when approached by a young person in need of advice about relationships. Your advice must be based on that which a good parent would give and it is important to consider the young person's emotional age as well as their chronological age. *Remember – you will have been approached by the young person for advice and not to make judgements*. They need to have confidence that they can have relationships without needing to be sexually active but if they are to be, then they should enter into them as informed as possible. Help them to consider the strength of the relationship they are in.

If despite such guidance it appears that the young person is likely to become sexually active or you find that they already are, then talk to them about the need for contraception, not just to prevent unwanted pregnancies but also to protect them from diseases. Again, information about agencies such as family planning clinics should be available so that the young person can be advised by a qualified counsellor and if appropriate, prescribed the most appropriate form of contraception for them, their age and lifestyle.

Check with your supervising social worker what to do in such cases. Inform the young person that these may be some of the issues that you will *have* to share with others. However, don't forget that the young person can receive confidential contraception advice and prescriptions if a GP feels they understand the implications and are competent. They do not need to have consulted with anyone else.

This is a summary of action for any carer of a young person who they know to be or believe to be sexually active and is either under age or considered vulnerable:

- Give the advice regarding the legal, moral and emotional issues – try not to judge them.
- Try to find out how much they know about contraception and safe sex and whether they are taking precautions.
- If they are not taking precautions, given them advice and information. Also give them information about agencies where they can discuss issues in more detail.
- Discuss the issue with your supervising social worker and the child's social worker.

Pregnancy

If a girl in your care becomes pregnant you should speak to them and tell them that you will have to inform their social worker. However, try to get the young person's consent. They are bound to feel very frightened, confused and unsure of themselves. They need to be given information to enable them to decide if they wish to proceed with the pregnancy, have a termination or consider adoption for the child. Again, it is important not to be judgmental or to have an adverse emotional response. You may feel protective towards the young person and you may also be angry. You must not let it affect your actions and support for the young person.

Getting treatment for sexually transmitted diseases/infectious diseases

There are many clinics and agencies that deal with sexually transmitted diseases. Ensure that you are aware of where they are and what they offer. Any young person in your care who is over the age of 16 may be treated confidentially. Be mindful that you are working as part of a team and that sometimes you will find that the expressed wishes of the young person run into conflict with this. Never promise anything to a young person if you feel that by doing so will put them at risk. Encourage them to seek help, even if it is within a confidential situation, i.e.; with a GP or a counsellor.

Young people, whether over 16 or under 16 years of age should not be put into a situation where they are made powerless or stripped of their dignity or ability to make choices or decisions.

In the event that the young person needs to be examined to exclude the contracting of a sexually transmitted disease, permission may be needed to allow the young person to be medically treated.

One of the things a young person may be frightened of is contracting AIDS. You should be confident that you are able to inform the young person of the differences between AIDS and VD (venereal diseases), as well as the difference between HIV and AIDS.

What is VD?

Venereal diseases (VD) are also known as sexually transmitted diseases (STD). They are transmitted not only through body fluids such as semen, vaginal fluid or blood but also saliva. Herpes for instance can be highly infectious and can be transmitted through close contact such as kissing and caressing – not just sexual intimacy.

Some VDs just give discomfort while others can be fatal if not treated. Most can be treated but it is especially important to ensure that any young person you are caring for is aware of how to protect themselves. They should also be encouraged to have medical checks if they are involved in unprotected sexual activity. This is especially important for girls or young women, as the symptoms may not be so immediately evident as they can be for boys or young men.

Some of the most common forms of VD include chlamydia, herpes, gonorrhea, genital warts, syphilis, hepatitis, crabs, and HIV.

It is worth saying that the government is determined to significantly lower the numbers of reported cases in young people of venereal diseases, especially chlamydia.

There has been a sharp increase in the reported incidents of VD so do not underestimate it.

What is HIV?

HIV (human immunodeficiency virus) is a sexually transmitted disease and the name of the virus that became widely known of in the early 1980s. It is known to attack the body's immune system, which then makes a person prone to infections and disease.

There are two ways that it can be passed on:

- Through sexual intercourse, both vaginal and anal.
- Through blood to blood contact. The two main routes here are via blood transfusions of unscreened blood and, more commonly by the sharing of needles when injecting drugs.

What is the difference between HIV and AIDS?

HIV is the initial stage of this virus. If a person is HIV positive, it does not mean that they have AIDS and nor is it now automatically assumed that they will get it. There are many developments in this field and the medical profession has managed to create drugs that have extended people's life expectancy dramatically. However, a diagnosis of HIV does need to be monitored and people may have to change their life style.

It is when a person has developed AIDS that they could be prone to dangerous secondary infections such as TB or pneumonia. AIDS itself does not kill a person but it weakens the person's immunity and creates the opportunity for other infections to be more potent or dangerous.

Young people who know they are HIV positive or that their parents are, or who have AIDS will need help and counselling. Young people with AIDS will also need a great deal of medical attention and guidance to conduct their lives in ways that will minimise any further risks to them or endanger others.

There are specialist agencies and clinics that can offer support and advice for the young person but also to enable you to support the young person.

If a child needing a placement has this diagnosis, then you will be told at the planning stage so that you can prepare yourself and your family. You will have to work out with your supervising social worker and the young person's social worker what you should tell your family and how they should respond to the young person. However, in general, if the young person is not infectious and unlikely to infect others then only a few people would need to know. Confidentiality and the prevention of a young person being stigmatised are very important in these instances.

Generally such a young person will already be linked into the medical profession who will be able to advise and guide you on how to care for the young person and what precautions you may need to take, if any. Your supervising social worker and the child's social worker will also be able to give guidance and advice. They will want the young person to experience as normal a family life as possible.

Your supervising social worker will also be able to help you to prepare your household and talk to your children with you. They may need to be given very clear and simple rules, as they would have if someone in your family was an epileptic or had diabetes. It is important that you feel confident to care for the young person. Your own protection and that of your family is equally important.

What is hepatitis?

Hepatitis is a virus that causes an infection of the liver. The infection can cause a serious illness although the majority of those infected fully recover. These viruses can be highly infectious and are contained in blood and body fluids so the routes of infection are similar to those of HIV. Control and prevention of infection to other people depends similarly on the adherence to the standards of hygiene you would follow for HIV and other infectious diseases.

The three main types of viral hepatitis are A, B and C. Speak to your supervising social worker for more information. Alternatively many health centres and GP's surgeries have information and there are many useful websites.

Alcohol, drugs and solvent abuse

Many young people will have experimented with alcohol, drugs and solvents from quite early ages. Adolescence is a time of experimentation and rebellion. However, young people from disrupted and unhappy backgrounds are more prone and susceptible to experimenting and then becoming hooked into using these drugs.

When dealing with these drugs you should not forget that the taking of drugs and the drinking of alcohol under the age of 16 in your house should not be permitted. You should at all times ensure that alcohol, drugs and aerosols are either locked away or where appropriate, used under supervision.

Solvent abuse and symptoms

Solvent abuse or 'glue sniffing' as it is commonly known can be highly dangerous and has been known to kill young children very early into their use of solvents. Children as young as 8-9 years of age can start to 'sniff glue' and they are able to do so as ordinary household items can be used. Parents, schools, shop keepers etc are more aware of this possibility and have responsibilities to prevent the abuse by refusing to give young people access to these products if they suspect they are being abused.

The products used include:

- butane gas – as used in cigarette lighters and refill cans
- liquid shoe polish
- dry cleaning fluids
- correcting fluid (Tipp-ex etc)
- highlighter and marker pens
- aerosols or spray can
- petrol

Specific solvent abuse symptoms

The main ranges of symptoms are those similar to alcohol and drug abuse (see below). However, remember that these lists are for guidance only and may have other causes, not least, in some cases, 'typical' teenage behaviour. If you have concerns, you must speak to the young person's social worker and your supervising worker. There are a number of areas from which you can obtain free advice.

Specific symptoms to look out for are as follows:

- Containers of substances and or plastic bags lying in places the young person uses.
- A smell of chemicals on the young person's clothes or breath.
- Behaviour as for drugs but more pronounced and more prone to violence.

Drugs and symptoms

There are many types of drugs and new drugs are being manufactured, some specifically to satisfy those who take drugs recreationally. There are many names and nicknames for the common drugs used. These change frequently with fashion as do the 'popular' drugs that are used. The most common types of drugs are as follows:

- amphetamines/stimulants – known as speed, whizz
- ecstasy – known as E, Dove
- cocaine – known as coke, charlie
- crack – made from cocaine, known as rocks
- cannabis – known as grass, weed, dope, marijuana, pot
- tranquillisers
- LSD – known as acid
- heroin

Known symptoms of drug abuse:

- Mood swings/can suddenly flare up/prone to depression/extreme introversion or extroversion.
- Inability to be coherent/speak clearly.
- Giggly/touchy.
- Starts suddenly becoming secretive and lying convincingly.
- Short-term memory loss.
- Starts avoiding eye contact.
- Filter paper/broken cigarettes/card lying about.
- Silver foil/razor blades lying about.
- Unexplained amounts of money going missing/the young person having debts.
- Having 'new friends'/abandoning existing friendship network.
- Sleeping a lot and then waking up 'dozy'.

Alcohol abuse and symptoms

Specific alcohol abuse symptoms:
Many symptoms are the same as symptoms for drug abuse. Initially the smell of alcohol can be clearly detected although a young person can learn to disguise the smell in time. The obvious signs would be known drunken behaviour and with bottles of alcohol in the room, but also look out for drinks going missing in your household.

Chapter 22

Contact

Contact

The fostering service makes sure that each child or young person in foster care is encouraged to maintain and develop family contacts and friendships as set out in her/his care plan and/or foster placement agreement.

NMS 10.1

NMS The National Minimum Standards also say the *fostering service* must ensure that:

- Clearly set out procedures for children in foster care to ensure that a child's contact is maintained, monitored and reviewed (**NMS 10.2**).
- When they are looking for or are putting forward suitable foster placements, the needs and benefits of contact for the child are considered at that stage. If the placement is found which is outside the child's area, then all involved should ensure that contact is supported (**NMS10.3**).
- Not only is the foster child asked for their views but that they are really considered when making contact arrangements (**NMS 10.4**).
- The importance of contact is emphasised from the outset for carers when they are being assessed and undergoing the preparation training and that the training underlines and develops the skills required from foster carers to enable them to encourage and facilitate contact (**NMS 10.5**).
- The local authority social worker must ensure before contact takes place, that a risk assessment is carried out, with clear arrangements made for any supervision that may be needed. A risk assessment is necessary unless there is an overriding requirement – i.e. a court order (**NMS 10.6**).
- The carer is supported and helped to deal with difficult contact issues and should ensure that the foster carer's role in supporting contact is clearly recorded in the Foster Placement Agreement (**NMS 10.7**).
- Financial support, transport or other costs are also offered to foster carers to ensure that contact takes place at the most suitable place and frequency (**NMS 10.8**).
- The foster carer makes clear recordings of the contact and what they think was the effect of the contact on the child and this information must be fed back to the child's social worker (**NMS 10.9**).

> **UKNS** The UK National Standards for Foster Care also include the following:
>
> - That the child's social worker, having consulted the foster carer, the child and the child's family and friends, co-ordinates all the contact arrangements, which includes the frequency and location and any supervision which may be necessary (**UKNS 9.4**).
> - That all involved give particular attention to contact arrangements where a child is particularly at risk of losing contact with specific aspects of their heritage (**UKNS 9.6**).
> - That the courts and other children's hearings are informed of the obligations placed on carers in meeting the contact arrangements set out for children in their care (**UKNS 9.8**).
> - That the carer has full details for all contacts listed in the child's care plan (**UKNS 9.9**).

What does this mean for you?

A young person's right to contact

It must always be seen that a child/young person has a right to contact with their parents, siblings or anyone important to them unless there is an over-riding safety reason for them not doing so. As a foster carer, you must actively encourage and support the children and young people to keep memories of their family alive. However, it is not just their immediate family. Children live as part of a wider network and many in their network may be equally important to them. They may also be very fond of pets that have been left behind.

Children you are caring for may not find it easy to tell you that they want to see their parents or their previous carers. They may think this might upset or anger you or that somehow they must not talk about them. This applies to older children as well as the younger ones. Keep the notion of contact as an open subject between yourself. For younger children you may think of games or books you could use that could help here.

Equally, a child/young person may indicate through their actions or words that they do not want contact. This is one of the things you will have to directly deal with but it is not usually good to encourage young people to sever all their contacts completely. We are all angry with our parents/carers, at some time in our lives and especially if there has been a major disruption during the earlier part of our lives. However, this does not mean that contact should cease. In all circumstances, the Children Act states that care and consideration should be given to seeking the views and wishes of the children you care for as you are likely to be closest to them, and you may be the best person to clarify these (**NMS 10.4**). You will need to show the young person that it is normal to be angry with our parents/siblings and that we may not want to see them at any one point. However, they nevertheless remain important in our lives. Encourage different forms of contact such as phone calls, letters, photos etc. It may be necessary to make separate contact arrangements for different members of the child's network.

You will need to discuss such issues with your supervising social worker and the young person's social worker and build in strategies to work positively with the child or young person. There are various steps that can be taken to either improve contact arrangements or to monitor them so that the young person is cushioned from the effects they may be worried about. In any event, all contact arrangements *should* be monitored and reviewed (**NMS 10.2**). You should also keep records of your own involvement and the way you feel it has gone for the young person. Encourage the young person to write, draw or otherwise record their own account of what went on and their own wishes for future contact. These observations should always be fed back to the young person's social worker and they should have copies of these records (**NMS 10.9**).

Promoting safe and meaningful contact will have been one of the training areas you will have undergone during your preparation period (**NMS 10.5**). It is also one of the themes which will be covered regularly because it is one of the most important aspects of being 'looked after' for children. It is also an area that can pose many difficulties, even if contact is going well. It can be very difficult explaining to a young child why they cannot go back to their family or why someone who is suspected of abusing a young child cannot have contact.

Contact by parents and relatives

Only in exceptional circumstances will contact *not* be part of the plan for the young person. Therefore facilitating contact for, and on behalf of the young person, is one of the most vital jobs you will have. Details of contact, frequency, people concerned, venue and travel arrangements will all be discussed at the placement planning meeting stage if not before and will have been part of the care plan (**NMS 10.2**). These contact arrangements should also be monitored and reviewed to ensure that they are still serving the young person's best interest.

As a general rule, contact should be facilitated at the foster carer's house unless there are reasons against this. Many of the older children will want to go to see their parents on their own and this may be encouraged if supervision is not necessary. Younger or more vulnerable children need to either be taken or supervised during their contact. You will be given information and guidance specific to the young person you are caring for and must ensure that contact complies with this. Your fostering agency will help you to facilitate these arrangements especially if the young person is placed outside of their normal area (**NMS 10.3**) and if contact arrangements are problematic or difficult (**NMS 10.7**).

Other ways of promoting contact

Working with the parent of a child you are looking after poses challenges. Encourage parents, where this is part of a care plan to participate as fully into their child's day-to-day life with you as possible. Consider activities like:

- bathing the child and putting them to bed
- reading them a story/helping them to read
- taking them shopping for their school uniform etc
- cooking them a meal
- attending sports days/parents evenings/school plays/assembly

All these activities of course will need to have been approved by the child's social worker. The assessment they will have to undertake (**NMS 10.6**) will consider what risks may be posed by contact and whether contact will need to be supervised or not.

What is supervised contact?

Supervised contact occurs when the local authority feels that it is too risky to allow unsupervised contact because they may fear the safety of the children or need to monitor the interaction of the parents and children. If you are asked to supervise contact you must be clear what you are being specifically asked to supervise and it must be made clear to the family what your role is. The child's social worker should be working with the parents to prepare them for the supervised contact.

It may be possible to undertake supervised contact in your home but more than likely it would take place in a neutral place for instance in a contact centre or nursery etc. It is also likely that if the contact is to take place outside your home for the contact to be supervised by someone else designated by the child's social worker or others advocating on behalf of the child.

Working with parents/parental responsibility

You should always remember that the parents of the young person you are caring for would always retain their parental responsibility towards the young person unless that young person is adopted. Therefore, even if the local authority has a full care order on the young person, their parents will still retain parental responsibility. In the latter case, however, the parents will share the parental responsibility with the local authority.

The concept of partnership with parents was established in the Children Act (1989) and this means that there are clear duties and responsibilities you will have as a foster carer to promote working in partnership and to promote the best for the child/young person you are caring for. However, except when there is a clear requirement, e.g. a court order, the fostering service cannot allow contact to take place until the child's social worker has undertaken a risk assessment and it is clear what supervision arrangements are necessary (**NMS 10.6**).

Parental responsibility can also be shared with:

- A guardian to the young person.
- A person delegated by the child's parents.
- A person who has been granted a residence order on the young person (foster carers can obtain this in some circumstances).
- The local authority if they are granted an emergency protection order (as well as when they have obtained a care order).

The child's father *will not* automatically have parental responsibility over his child but will do so if:

- He was married to the child's mother at the time of the birth or subsequently.
- He applies to the court for parental responsibility.

- The child's mother formally recognises him as the father and this is registered in the High Court.
- The child's father asks to be made a guardian to the young person.
- He is granted a residence order.

Parents *must* be informed and consulted and their views and wishes regarding their child must be considered. In situations where parental responsibility is shared, the local authority will try to come to an agreement with the parents on any particular course of action it feels is right for the child.

When sharing parental responsibility, consultation is important, however, ultimately, those sharing parental responsibility with the parent(s), i.e. the local authority, will have the overriding responsibility.

Social work visits

Social workers must visit all children who are looked after within certain timeframes. Below are the statutory *minimum* requirements for social worker visits:

- Within the first week
- Placements up to a year: every 6 weeks
- After the first year: every three months

Under regulations the social worker should see the child alone and you must ensure that the opportunities to do so are encouraged. The social worker should also undertake an unannounced visit on the child and their household and this can take place at any (reasonable) time.

Chapter 23

Education

The education of children looked after

The fostering service gives a high priority to meeting the educational needs of each child or young person in foster care and ensures that she/he is encouraged to attain her/his full potential.

NMS 13.1

NMS The National Minimum Standards also say the *fostering service* must ensure that:

- They give a high priority to helping carers to ensure that each child they look after reaches their educational potential or goes beyond it (**NMS 13.2**).
- Carers are to actively contribute to the assessment of a child's educational needs as well as the planning and reviewing of the assessment. Carers should also be involved in the development of a child's personal education plan (**NMS 13.3**).
- Carers are clear about what is required of them when getting involved with the child's school and what *they* should do, what the birth parent may do and what they may be involved with together. That this is set out in the care plan for the child and includes activities such as; parents evenings, open days and discussions with teachers (**NMS 13.4**).
- The foster home is one that:
  - promotes, encourages and values education
  - is clear that schooling is important and that children should attend regularly
  - enables the child to be fully part of the school by ensuring that they are provided with the necessary uniform, equipment and financial or other support to attend school trips or after school activities
  - supports the child with their homework (**NMS 13.5**).
- The foster placement agreement form identifies clearly who should pay for school costs, including school uniform, school trips and equipment (**NMS 13.8**).
- Fostering agencies must keep information on how the child or young person has done at school and the details of those who are excluded (**NMS 13.6**).
- Fostering agencies must also have arrangements and clear expectations about what they will put in place if any child is not in school. These arrangements must include 'structured occupation' (**NMS 13.7**).

Education **83**

> **UKNS** The UK National Standards for Foster Care also include the following:
>
> - That authorities involved in providing educational services give a high priority to promoting not just the quality of education but the continuity of it including providing professional support and extra tuition (**UKNS 11.1**). That opportunities for further or higher education, vocational training and employment are also actively encouraged (**UKNS 11.9**).
> - That the necessary people in an authority are notified of the child's placement in foster care and are also involved in the assessment, planning and review of the child's educational requirements (**UKNS 11.6**).
> - That in line with keeping records of a child's educational achievements, the fostering agencies hold statistical information which includes the child's:
>   - ethnic origin
>   - gender
>   - information about special needs/disability
>   - and that this information is used to look at making improvements to the services provided (**UKNS 11.7**).
> - That pre-school children should have access to day care provisions such as play groups or nurseries to promote their early learning and ability to be with other children and adults (**UKNS 11.8**).
> - That there is an effective way of handling bullying in school and that complaints about bullying are taken up without delay (**UKNS 11.10**).
> - That there are clear procedures for notifying when a child has been excluded from school (**UKNS 11.11**).

What does this mean for you?

All those involved with a child in foster care will seek a high commitment from carers to enable children to continue to attend their own school or to have their special educational needs met while they are staying with you. These factors will be discussed with you at the time of the referral and the agency will give such support as they can to enable this to continue (**NMS 13.2**). Your agency and the child's local authority will also provide support, resources and information to enable the placement to continue especially if the young person is out of full time education. If the child is to be out of school for any period, they should be provided with 'structured occupation during school hours' (**NMS 13.7**). Check resources are available and insist that any break from schooling the child might have is minimised.

These issues should be thoroughly explored during the placement planning meeting. If you feel you will have difficulties with the proposals you must say, so that the meeting has a clear idea of who is going to undertake what role for the young person to enable their education to continue. In some cases young people may have to change schools or receive a different service at, for instance a pupil referral unit.

You will be expected to fully contribute to the planning and reviewing of a child's educational needs and be involved in any work identified to you under the young person's personal education plan (PEP – see below) (**NMS 13.3**).

The role of the young person's social worker, the child's parent, and especially your role should be clearly defined at the meeting and there should be clear decisions as to who is going to do what and by when. There should be a clear understanding and agreement that includes contact with the school, attending parents meetings and attending other events at the school or college (**NMS 13.4**). Wherever possible, the young person's parent should be encouraged to take on some of these roles and you may be asked as a carer to encourage or go with them. Care should be taken to ensure that the young person has been consulted and that their views and wishes are considered.

The focus should not be just on the young person's academic achievements i.e. SATs but should also promote the non-academic activities such as sports. Encourage and be positive about the young person's abilities. It is also important to have a healthy expectation of what the young person can achieve. Remember that children who are looked after are significantly more likely than your own children to need support. Don't let them down by having low expectations of them (**NMS 13.5**).

Foster carers should be positive advocates and role models for young people and encourage children to see education as a positive right as well as an opportunity to be stimulated and stretched. They should be helped to understand that education can expand the opportunities they may have in later life by showing them what options are out there (**NMS 13.5**). Quite often, what restricts us is not knowing about things – it is vital that they see that there is a wider picture than just what their life may have presented them so far.

Make time on a regular basis to supervise the completion of the young person's homework and where literacy is a problem, encourage them to read by listening to them. It is also important for learning and self-esteem that the young person is encouraged to debate issues and express opinions. Showing an interest or introducing an element of fun can demonstrate to young people that homework is not always a chore. Be creative and try not to make doing homework a battleground.

The government's performance indicators for the education of looked after children

The government has set out achievement targets that it expects schools to achieve (or exceed) for all the pupils they have in their school who are looked after. These indicators have already been adjusted and your agency will advise you of the updated details. You will need to be familiar with these indicators so that you can ensure that the child or young person makes the most out of their opportunities. Your fostering agency will be keeping similar information on the children/young people (**NMS 13.6**).

Education plans

This is a measure introduced by the government to enhance educational opportunities and educational experiences for children who are looked after in the Personal Education Plan (PEP) see Chapter 15 *Looked After Children Documents*. Each school has a designated teacher who takes responsibility for the co-ordination of Personal Education Plans. Find out who the teacher is and keep in contact with them for advice or help as needed.

What are Personal Education Plans (PEPs)?

The Department of Health has found that care plans and children's reviews have not sufficiently promoted or prioritised the educational needs of children who are looked after. The Personal Education Plan (PEP) has been devised to remedy this. A PEP should ensure:

- The child has access to the necessary educational services and support they may need.
- That the services and support maximises the child's chances for stability by working to prevent disruptions or exclusions in school.
- The child's school needs are clearly assessed, this also includes addressing the needs of a child that may arise from being bullied at school.
- There are clear targets set for the child as well as all those working with them to ensure that the child is given the opportunities and encouragement to meet their educational potential.

The Personal Education Plan should also work as a record of the progress and the achievement of children and young people.

When should the Personal Education Plan start?

These plans are started by the child/young person's social worker and the agency or you may well be in the position of ensuring that it happens. They should be agreed as soon as is possible or at least within 20 days of the child being accommodated or of joining a new school. The PEP should be reviewed together with the Care Plan and specifically at the child's Looked After Reviews.

You can actively help to promote the child's educational needs by identifying who in the school is to help the young person to achieve the different objectives; who will offer guidance for the young person's career path for instance? The young person's own role in the plan and their views of the school should be an integral part of the plan.

When there is a possibility that a young person may be suspended or excluded from school or is just not getting on, the school should involve the young person in a pastoral support programme. This is a scheme designed to help the young person to manage their behaviour in an acceptable way. It is hoped that this programme will be able to identify young people who may need this intervention before things come to a head and exclusion becomes a possibility.

Your supervising social worker and the young person's social worker will be able to offer more advice and information to you.

What is my role as a carer?

As a carer for a child or young person you are expected to do what a 'good' parent would do for their own child. Whilst it is also true that children you are looking after *may* have more educational needs than your own, the expectations on you will follow similar paths as for your own children.

What a good parent or carer should do

- Ensure there is sufficient comfortable and quiet space to enable homework to be done.
- Attend all parents evenings and meetings to do with the child – this may involve working with the child's parent/guardian.

- Get to know their teacher, head of year or SENCO (Special Educational Needs Co-ordinator)
- Keep a school diary.
- Monitor homework and sign off the homework regularly.
- Have a clear culture in the home such as 'homework hour' when TV and computer games are banned, and be available to help with home work.
- Make it clear to the young person what you expect from them and what you feel they can achieve. This needs to be balanced so that a young person can achieve their potential but not get too stressed because the expectation is too high.
- *Basically – be a good parent*

Statement of Educational Needs

A Statement of educational needs is the result of an assessment of the child's needs within education. It is normally undertaken when it is clear that the child is unable to fully participate in the activities/lessons provided by the school.

The expectation on all schools is that they must have done everything they can do to help a child before considering this step. If the school has been able to identify needs that the child might have and is dealing with it, then the need to go down the 'statement' route may not be necessary.

What to do if you feel a child needs more help or is not coping

Close monitoring and close working with the child's teacher should ensure that the signs are being picked up. The child's parents will usually also be able to fill you in on crucial details.

As a carer, you cannot necessarily request an educational statement for the child but you should discuss this with the child's social worker who can ask for the process to start. The assessment will include a range of information from different sources which should create a complete picture of what is going on educationally for the child. You should be asked for your opinion and your own assessment of the child's needs.

Once this process is started it should take approximately six weeks to gather all the relevant information and then be presented to a Special Needs panel where decisions will be taken. Decisions can range from transferring the young person to a special school to keeping the young person in their current school and providing classroom support.

Should you need more information on this, your agency will have a copy of the Department of Education and Skills, Code of Practice on this.

Leisure activities

Most young people you will be caring for will have a poor self-image and your role includes promoting activities for them which give them opportunities to succeed and get a sense of achievement. Opportunities can range from games and sports, clubs; arts and crafts and other creative activities; music; dancing, cycling, swimming or to reading books to stimulate their interests and boost their sense of themselves. Get to know what is going on in your locality and consider how it may benefit the child or young person.

Chapter 24

Leaving Care/After Care

Leaving Care/After Care

The fostering service ensures that their foster care service helps to develop skills, competencies and knowledge necessary for adult living.

NMS 14.1

NMS The National Minimum Standards also say the fostering service must ensure that:

- They have clear and written guidelines that carers follow as they are preparing young people towards adult life (**NMS 14.2**).
- That carers receive the necessary support and training to prepare young people effectively for adult life (**NMS 14.3**).
- They work to enable the carers to be aware that the necessary skills should be learned from an early age and does not just rely on the age or the level of understanding the child presents (**NMS 14.4**).
- That young people are fully consulted about their future care and needs and are involved in making decisions for their pathway plans (**NMS 14.5**).

UKNS The UK National Standards for Foster Care also include the following:

- That local authorities have a clear and well publicised leaving care policy, which includes all the legal requirements, and that this is integrated into children's services plans and monitored and reviewed regularly (**UKNS 12.1**).
- That each young person leaving foster care is given a detailed guide to leaving care and that this is in the form that is easily understandable and includes how they can obtain continued support, advice and guidance (**UKNS 12.5**). Included in this are details of state benefits or other sources of financial support and that young people are helped to obtain 'sufficient' to maintain themselves (**UKNS 12.6**).
- Local authorities have good working practices with agencies such as housing, education, employment and training services and benefit providers and that this network works to support all children leaving foster care (**UKNS 12.7**).

→

- That young people should have a range of accommodation, some of them supported, from where they can maintain their links with their family, foster family, work and other important connections (**UKNS 12.9**).
- Carers should be supported, including financially, where they are able to support and care for young people who are in the process of leaving care and for a period immediately after they have left care (**UKNS 12.10**).
- All local authorities should monitor and evaluate the effectiveness of their services for children preparing for adult life and make sure that lessons are learnt and used to improve future services (**UKNS 12.11**).
- All young people with a disability must be specifically identified with all the connecting services such as health and education and special care and attention must be paid when preparing them for adult life (**UKNS 12.8**).

Preparing young people for adult life is a significant function for any foster carer. Ideally, the child or young person should be being prepared from the start of any placement, as you would with your own children in order to prepare them to stand on their own feet. Young people who have been looked after represent a significant percentage of those who end up homeless, in prison or as those on benefits or in poorly paid jobs. In recognition of this and in an attempt to address this, the government has introduced legislation (see below), which should make your role and responsibility clearer when preparing young people for a more rewarding adult life.

The Act says:
> *The main purpose of the Children (Leaving Care) Act 2000 is to improve the life chances of young people living in and leaving local authority care. Its main aims are: to delay young people's discharge from care until they are prepared and ready to leave; to improve the assessment, preparation and planning for leaving care; to provide better personal support for young people after leaving care; and to improve the financial arrangements for care leavers.*
>
> Extracts from the Regulations and Guidance – Children (Leaving Care) Act 2000

What does this mean for you?

The Act states that where any young person is looked after the agency has a duty 'to advise, assist and befriend her/him with a view to promoting his welfare' in preparation for when they leave the placement. *This is also your role.*

Independent fostering agencies do not have a legal duty to provide after care for the young person once they have left but it is imperative that you equip a young person as well as you can for their life ahead. Your agency has a duty to inform the local authority if a young person aged 16 or older is leaving foster care and this should be done with as much notice as possible to enable the local authority to provide the necessary support and resources.

Connexions (*England only*)

Connexions was introduced in some areas from 2001 and is a service aimed at providing advice and support to all young people aged 13-19 but with priority to those who are the most vulnerable and therefore less likely to make a good transition into adult life. It aims to ensure that all young people have the opportunities to learn skills that will equip them into adult life and beyond. It advocates that young people should be stretched and that their carers should have high but realistic expectations of them so that they are able to continue into education or take up useful employment (**NMS 14.2**).

There will be personal advisors who help young people through this process and they will be attached to the local authority leaving care service. There will also be Connexions advisors who will have similar responsibilities but with some variations.

Transition into adult life

Your agency must have clear written procedures of what is expected of foster carers in terms of preparing children and young people for leaving care and these should be updated regularly. Foster carers should also receive training and support to enable them to be actively involved in the leaving care/pathway plans for the young person they are caring for (**NMS 14.3**). This includes the need for carers to provide and train the young person in the life skills necessary to prepare for adult life and to provide them with opportunities to attain these skills both inside and outside the home (**NMS 14.4**).

Children and young people should always be consulted on their views and wishes regarding their future, and this would include their pathway plans (**NMS 14.5**). Carers are actively encouraged to enable the young person to discuss their fears, anxieties and excitement about what they wish for themselves.

Practice issues

The Children (Leaving Care Act) Guidance says that: 'services for young people must take account of the lengthy process of transition from childhood to adulthood ... and that the support provided should, broadly, be the support that a 'good parent' might be expected to give.' All agencies including education, housing, health and leisure should be working together in a way that the child and their family can understand so that they can access the necessary resources. All local authorities should have a guide for young people informing them of the services available to them. This should inform how the local authority proposes to meet the requirements of young people's pathway plans. These guides should distinguish between the services they will provide and those that are available through the private sector.

How should we all be working to prepare young people?

The Guidance (Page 3) sets out a list, which although the responsibility of local authorities, shows how we should all be working together to promote and provide the following:

1. Stable placements, continuity of carers and the maintenance, wherever possible, of positive links with people who are important to the child or young person whilst the young people are 'looked after'.

2. 'Look after' young people until they are prepared and ready to leave care.
3. Promote and maintain relationships with carers and families, where possible, after young people leave care.
4. Prepare young people gradually to be ready to leave care, paying attention to practical self-care needs – health, budgeting, domestic skills – and personal and relationship dimensions.
5. Enable young people leaving care to fulfil their potential in education, training and employment.
6. Ensure young people leaving care have access to a range of accommodation and the support and skills to maintain themselves in their accommodation.
7. Ensure that there is a contingency provision to support care leavers in the event of a crisis, including arrangements for respite.
8. Provide or enable on-going personal support. This may include support by specialist leaving care scheme support, support by carers and social workers, and support by youth workers, befrienders, mentors or volunteers. This is underlined by the introduction of personal advisers under the 2000 Leaving Care Act.
9. Where young people leaving care are entitled to claim welfare benefits, ensure that they receive their full entitlements.
10. Involve young people in all assessment, planning, review and decision-making for leaving care.
11. Inform young people leaving care of the available services – including the provision of accessible leaving care guides – and of their right to access their own records.
12. Monitor and evaluate outcomes of 1-11 above.

What should carers be doing to prepare young people?

The Leaving Care Act 2000 identifies the following skills young people should be equipped with:

- How to shop for, prepare and cook food.
- Understanding of a balanced diet.
- Laundry, sewing and mending and other housekeeping skills.
- How to carry out basic household jobs such as mending fuses (which will involve basic electrical and other knowledge).
- Safety in the home and first aid.
- The cost of living.
- Household budgeting, including the matching of expenditure to income, the regular payment of bills and avoidance of the excessive use of credit.
- Health education, including personal hygiene.
- Sexual education, including contraception and preparing for parenthood.
- Applying, and being interviewed for a job.
- The rights and responsibilities of being an employee.
- The rights and responsibilities of being an employer (disabled young people may use direct payments to employ their own personal assistants).
- Applying for a course of education or training.
- Applying for housing and locating and maintaining it.
- Registering with a doctor and dentist.
- Knowledge of emergency services (fire, police, ambulance).

- Finding and using community services and resources.
- Contacting the social services department and other caring agencies
- Contacting organisations and groups set up to help young people who are, or have been in care.
- The role of agencies such as Citizens' Advice Bureau, local councillors and MPs.
- How (a) to obtain advice; (b) how to write a letter of complaint.

What is a pathway plan?

The pathway plan is the plan that starts the active preparation of a child towards adult life and independence.

Pathway planning

When should pathway planning begin?

The Leaving Care Act says that 'preparation for this process should be incorporated in the care plan for the young person as soon as they start to be looked after, accommodated or privately fostered'. There is much emphasis on the preparation for the pathway plans and much encouragement that planning starts well ahead of time. All children, no matter how young, should be taught to take responsibilities appropriate to their age and development and should be encouraged to learn domestic and social skills. However, an assessment cannot be finalised until the young person has reached their 16th birthday. As carers you should in any event be planning with the young person for this process and the Assessment and Progress Records are useful here. The Integrated Children Scheme will create some changes; see your supervising social worker for further details and also Chapter 15.

What should be included in the assessment of a pathway plan?

- The young person's health and development.
- Their needs for education, training or employment.
- The support available to them from their family and other relationships.
- Their financial needs.
- The extent to which they possess the practical and other skills necessary for independent living.
- Their needs for care, support and accommodation.

There is a clear requirement that on-going support can be provided to the young person up to the age of 21 or where relevant beyond, until the agreed end of the programme.

The content of the pathway plan

1. Personal support: to be given by a personal advisor from the Connexions Service. The personal support to a young person leaving care will include practical issues such as ensuring the young person has a National Insurance Number. The personal advisors also have a central co-ordinating role.
2. Accommodation.

3. Education and training.
4. Employment.
5. Family and social relationships.
6. Practical and other skills.
7. Financial support.
8. Health needs.
9. Contingency planning.

When should the pathway plans be reviewed?

Pathway plans should be reviewed at the request of the young person, their personal adviser or at least every six months.

Role of the personal advisors

The local authority should arrange for each eligible and relevant child to have a personal advisor. The role of the personal adviser is:

- To provide advice (including practical advice) and support.
- To participate in the assessment and preparation of the pathway plan.
- To participate in reviews of the pathway plan.
- To liaise with the responsible authority in the implementation of the pathway plan.
- To co-ordinate the provisions of services and to take reasonable steps to ensure that the young person makes use of such services.
- To keep informed about the child's progress and well being.
- To keep written records of contact with the child.

Chapter 25

Managing a Child's Behaviour

Managing behaviour

Training for foster carers includes training in caring for a child who has been abused, safe caring skills, managing behaviour and recognising signs of abuse and on ways of boosting and maintaining the child's self-esteem.

NMS 9.2

> **NMS** The National Minimum Standards also say the *fostering service* must ensure that:
>
> Managing young people's behaviour is an acknowledged challenge for all parents and therefore an important issue for foster carers to consider in relation to the children they foster. You will all have your own house rules and safe caring documents and have different expectations of the kind of behaviour you find acceptable or unacceptable. Make sure that the young person knows and understand what the house rules and safe caring rules are (**NMS 9.3**). The management of young people's behaviour is one of the aspects of fostering for which there will be training available which you must attend. This section is intended to give you some general guidance.

Methods of control and discipline

The Children Act 1989 states that the following forms of punishment *are not* permitted when caring for children looked after:

- Corporal punishment, including any intentional application of force such as slapping, pinching, squeezing, shaking, throwing missiles and rough handling. It includes punching or pushing in the heat of the moment and in response to violence from the young person. It does not, however, prevent a carer from taking necessary physical action to prevent danger or personal injury, injury to the young person or another person or to avoid damage to property.
- Withholding of food, drink, and medicines; this should be taken to include access to the amounts and range of food or drinks normally available to children.
- Restricting contacts with the family, social workers or people who are important to the young person.

All carers must have a clear idea of what is considered reasonable discipline and this is something which should be discussed with your supervising social worker.

You may already use sanctions with your own children. You need to discuss with your supervising social worker what these sanctions are and consider if they can be the same for the young person you are caring for. The use of sanctions should be discussed very early on and must be agreed by the young person's social worker. Similarly, there should be a clear understanding as to how disputes and fights between foster children or between your own children and foster children are to be dealt with. You should be mindful that you should be recording such incidents.

What does this mean for you?

When should you use physical restraint?

Physical restraint should never be used as a punishment and should only be used in exceptional circumstances:

- To prevent a serious risk of harm to the child or other persons.
- To prevent serious damage to property.

(You should not use physical restraint to force a child or young person to do something where there is no immediate risk to them, to others or to property.)

What to try in order to minimise the need for physical restraint

- Always try to pre-empt possible trigger points for a young person, reassure them or divert them from tensions.
- Try to divert the child's attention or lead them away from a conflict situation.
- Be mindful of what you know about the child/young person, it may give you a clue as to how you may get them to calm down.
- Make it clear to the young person that you may have to use restraint, or call for help if the behaviour continues.

If you do need to use physical restraint

- Use only the minimum necessary force to prevent injury or damage and use care to avoid intimate parts of the body.
- The person using the restraint should preferably be the person who knows the young person the best or has a good relationship with them. They should be talking to the young person, explaining what they are doing and trying to calm them down throughout.
- Where at all possible, get a witness to the event. Talk the child through what is happening and try to calm them down.
- Once the child is calming down, the restraint should be relaxed and the child allowed to regain their self-control and dignity.

Make sure you record and report all incidents as soon as possible to your supervising social worker.

Encouraging positive behaviour

In order to learn how to behave, young people should know what is expected of them and to know that someone cares enough that they do behave. A lot of this is based on trust. Sometimes a young person will present challenges right from the start and at other times they will do so after the 'honeymoon period' is over. The young person will look to you and your family for clear boundaries and consistency in responses to things. They will see you and other adults as role models. Always try to reward or remark on positive behaviour and enforce positive attention seeking. Young people need your approval but they also need honest disapproval of their behaviour which makes clear that it is the behaviour that is unacceptable and not the young person themselves.

You should have clarified with your supervising social worker what your own strategies are for managing behaviour but one of the useful methods is to consider the *ABC* method which considers these three components:

- Antecedents: what sets the young person off, i.e. what is the trigger for the behaviour?
- Background: where and when does it get set off?
- Consequences: what is the result, i.e. what is the pay off for the young person?

Understanding the personality and history of the young person is vital in any coping strategy so don't jump to conclusions or assume responses from the young person. Listen to what is going on and how it is being done. Prioritise some aspects of behaviour and set base lines for yourself and them as to what constitutes dangerous or illegal behaviour. A useful guide is the Fostering Network's (NFCA) booklet on 'Managing Behaviour'.

Agree with your supervising social worker and the young person's social worker what you are going to work on with the young person in terms of behaviour modification. It is better to concentrate on one aspect of a young person's behaviour than to end up criticising and challenging all of it as this is unlikely to lead to any improvements, either in the child/young person's behaviour or in the situation as a whole.

Understanding your own reactions and responses

Knowing how *you* react to particular situations is important and wherever possible, try to work closely with your partner/spouse so that you can deal with the situation in as safe and constructive way as possible. You need to remain in control of the situation and to help the young person to develop self-control and insight into their behaviour. This is very difficult for young people to learn as they have probably had to respond in the same way for a long time. They may also have much pent up anger, some of which they will not be able to readily identify the roots of. It is therefore important for the young person to learn to feel safe to release some of these strong emotions in a strong and supportive foster home.

Try to mark out different roles with your partner so that you can both support each other. Know what your own trigger points are and get your partner or supporter to help in these circumstances. As previously mentioned, this is a very difficult and challenging aspect of caring and your fostering agency should offer training and support both generally and specifically on this subject.

Chapter 26

When a Child is Missing From Home

When a child/young person is missing from home

The fostering service makes sure that the foster carer has a clear written procedure for use if the foster child is missing from home.

NMS 9.8

A missing child is an extremely worrying situation for all those who care for children and foster carers need to be prepared in advance for what they should do in such circumstances. To a certain extent, it depends on the age and understanding of a child. For example, if a young child or a child with learning difficulties disappears from your care, then you should be actively seeking them and alerting others as soon as you realise they are missing. In the case of an older child or young person who is able to go out unaccompanied by an adult, it is possible to allow them some leeway if they do not return home at an agreed time. It is also sensible to check that they are not with family or friends if you can do so. However, err on the side of caution as foster children, particularly if they are unfamiliar with the area in which you live, must be considered as vulnerable.

Try to plan ahead for such an incident by always having a clear agreement with a child about what they should do for instance, if they get lost. There should also be clear agreements about where the child is going and who they are going to be with. If a child has a mobile phone, ensure that it is charged and there is enough credit to be able to contact each other.

If you have looked for the child or contacted people in the places they are likely to be but have not been able to find the child, then you must report the child as missing. Your agency will have clear guidance on who you should contact first. In some instances, if you phone your fostering agency, they will report the child missing to the police. In other cases, they will ask you to do so. The child's social worker or their local authority will also need to be notified. If they are unavailable then you should ask to speak to their manager or someone else in authority. If this happens out of office hours, then you will need to contact the emergency duty system for the local authority which has placed the child. This telephone number should be given to you when the child is first placed.

The police will ask you details of the child. They may do this over the phone or visit you to take details and will need to know what the child was wearing and, if possible, to have a recent photograph. Failing this, they will need a detailed physical description of the child. The police may need to search your house and garden as they have to check out all possibilities.

Usually the child or young person will turn up safe and well and will then be collected from wherever they are. If they have run away, the police will probably want to interview the child or young person to make sure nothing has happened in their present placement to make them do this. If a young person returns of their own volition, do not forget to notify the police and others that they have returned.

When a child is missing, whatever the circumstances, it is an extremely distressing time. Once the child has returned safely, it is essential to look at this situation preferably with the child or young person, the child's social worker and your supervising social worker in order to try to work out why it happened and ways to minimise the possibility of it happening again.

Ensure that you keep detailed records of what happened in the period leading up to a young person being missing or where you had suspected this might happen. Recording the event and the time is particularly important. Below is some further guidance on what to do when a child goes missing.

Before reporting a child as missing

- Contact the last place the young person should have been at – school, work, friends etc.
- Check with friends/relatives/colleagues when the young person was last seen.
- Check if the young person has taken clothes, other possessions and money or any other signs that indicate that this is a deliberate action.

If you need to report to the police that the young person is missing make sure you have the following information at hand:

- Full name and any nicknames the young person is known as.
- Date of birth.
- Ethnicity/racial origin.
- Skin, hair, eye colouring and any distinguishing features, i.e. style of hair cut, glasses etc.
- Height/weight.
- Distinguishing features.
- Whether the young person needs or is likely to need medical treatment or suffers for instance from diabetes, asthma.
- Clothing/jewellery the young person may be wearing.
- Date/time of absence and the circumstances.
- Last known place the young person was/or was supposed to be.
- Any areas/friends the young person is likely to have gone to.
- The young person's legal status/name of social worker/local authority.

Again, as with all lists, this is not exhaustive. Basically, you should pass on any information that will help locate and return the young person.

If there is a fear that the child has been or is likely to be abused by you or a member of your family, then the child will not be returned to you and investigations will commence (see Chapter 20 *Child Protection* and Chapter 28 *Children Making Complaints*).

How to respond when the young person returns

Not returning home at the right time will be difficult for the young person to reconcile. They may be frightened or angry and fear your anger or rejection. It is important to consider your response to the young person carefully. You may be angry or have been frightened yourself but you must make sure that your own responses do not aggravate the situation. It is best to welcome the young person into your home, assure yourself that they are well and unharmed. Establish whether they are hungry or in need of a wash or need to sleep etc. Tell them that you were concerned and that you would like to talk to them about this when you are both over the heat of the incident/rested and more relaxed.

It is useful to discuss your feelings with your supervising social worker who would be able to advise on ways of talking with the young person aimed at building bridges. Something like this could lead to better dialogue with the young person and a breakthrough in your relationship with them. It is important to consider the circumstances of this episode, understand what happened and build in contingencies to minimise re-occurrence.

However, please remember to notify all the agencies, individuals etc. that the child is back and safe – they too will be worried!

Chapter 27

Bullying

The fostering service ensures that foster carers are aware of the particular vulnerability of looked after children and their susceptibility to bullying and procedures are in place to recognise, record and address any instance of bullying and to help foster carers cope with it.

NMS 9.6

This issue is becoming more recognised with schools (and other agencies) having and imposing anti-bullying policies. Unhappily however, bullying is prevalent but, once bullying is recognised, it becomes more difficult for the bully to 'get away with it' for very long. Those who are vulnerable can be spotted and helped to protect themselves and we can also arm ourselves with information about those who may be bullies.

Children and young people are no different from adults in their fear of being a 'snitch' or a 'grass' but if they can be confident that they will not only be listened to but that this will be a positive thing to do, they are more likely to report incidents.

If you feel that a young person you are caring for is either the victim of bullying or vulnerable to it, you must speak to the young person's social worker and your supervising social worker.

School is an important aspect of a child's life and therefore it is important that you build good working relationships with the young person's school so that you can work together to protect the young person or to empower them to help themselves.

What is bullying?

Bullying is a deliberate act of hostility or aggression against someone aimed at causing pain and distress and a situation that allows one person to use their power or strength over someone in a lesser position. Bullying can show itself in different ways, for example:

- **Physical:** pushing, punching, pinching – any use of violence.
- **Verbal:** calling names, teasing, deliberately misleading, sarcasm.
- **Emotional:** tormenting, threatening, being rude and unfriendly, gestures.
- **Racist:** racial taunts and threats.
- **Sexual:** rude and abusive comments, unwanted physical contact.
- **Homophobic:** taunts and threats, spreading rumours.

Why do some children bully?

Some young children may use bullying behaviour because they may have:

- Learned that bullying had been a way of getting things they may otherwise not have been able to get.

- Thought that they could get away with it and that no-one would challenge them.
- Become a powerful member or leader in a group.
- Find that it helps them to divert or mask personal difficulties they may have.

Signs that a child may be bullied

- Suddenly be frightened or reluctant to undertake outside activities previously enjoyed or undertaken regularly i.e. going to a club, attending school.
- Lack confidence, self-esteem, become withdrawn.
- Become easily distressed or tearful.
- Ask for more money or starts stealing.
- Unable to explain about bruises, cuts or getting into fights etc.

Some of the long-term consequences of being bullied

- Depression, low self-esteem, sense of guilt, sense of shame.
- Fear of meeting new people, going into new places, social isolation.
- Agoraphobia, anxiety/panic attacks.
- Could use bullying behaviour on their own close ones including children, siblings.
- Become suicidal.

Guidance on tackling bullying

- All cases of bullying should be reported and recorded – do not ignore it.
- Reassure the child that it is not their fault and make specific time to talk to them about their day and how they are feeling.
- Help the child to practice walking in a confident manner.
- Help the child to shout 'NO' loudly and confidently.
- Advise the child to stay within a group and not become isolated.

How to work with the school

Make sure that you have been making notes on what the foster child has been telling you and what you have observed. These details will form the basis of your discussions with the child's school. Check the school has an anti-bullying policy. This policy should explain how to take your concerns further and how the school will work with you to ensure the safety of the child. Go to see the head teacher and work out an agreed way of tackling this matter.

Ensure you have your agency procedures for tackling bullying and that you understand them.

Chapter 28

Children Making Complaints

Making a complaint

The fostering service ensures that children in foster care know how to raise any concerns or complaints, and ensures that they receive prompt feed back on any concerns or complaints raised.

NMS 11.5

Children and young people, their parents, foster carers and other people involved are able to make effective representations, including complaints, about any aspect of the fostering service, whether it is provided directly by an authority or by a contracted authority or agency.

UKNS 25

NMS The National Minimum Standards also say the *fostering service* must ensure that:

- All fostering agencies must produce a Statement of Purpose which sets out the aims and objectives of their fostering service and has systems in place to ensure they meet the aims and objectives (**NMS 1**). The statement of purpose must include clear details about how to complain about the fostering service (**NMS 1.4** and **22.8**).
- All fostering agencies must also produce a 'children's guide' which should be accessible to all children they look after and which should contain details of the services offered to them by the agency and the standards they should expect. A very clear part of the children's guide must contain information on how children may complain or raise issues about any aspect of their care (**NMS 1.5**).
- They keep records about complaints which should be stored separately and securely (**NMS 25.2**) but are clearly recorded on the relevant files for staff, carers and children. This must include the conclusions and actions taken and the fostering agency must keep information that brings details of all complaints and allegations together so that these are reviewed and the necessary lessons learnt (**NMS 25.13**).

UKNS The UK National Standards in Foster Care also include the following:

- That any person making a complaint or representation knows that they can call upon independent support for any relevant meeting or discussion (**UKNS 25.6**).
- That those who have made a complaint receive a copy of the outcome within an agreed time limit set out in the agency's complaints procedure (**UKNS 25.7**).

→

- That each agency publishes an annual report on all the complaints and other issues that have been raised with them about the service they have provided, with details of the procedures they followed and the outcomes reached (**UKNS 25.9**).
- That the procedures for complaints and representations state that agencies must make specific arrangements for people whose first language is not English and those whose disability may make use of the procedures difficult (**UKNS 25.5**).

What does this mean for you?

Helping young people to complain

All children and young people have the right to complain and information about how to complain should be given to them in a clear and understandable form. Information about making a complaint should not just be from their local authority but also from the fostering agency, as they should be clear just what their rights in foster care are. They should be made aware of the standard and range of care they should expect from their placement. This information will be contained in the Children's Guide that all fostering agencies must ensure is given to the child and their family when the child is looked after.

All young people who wish to make a complaint should be encouraged and supported. You will find that if a young person has confided in you or a member of your family then you should act as an advocate for them. There are delicate balances to strike here as it is important that the process of making a complaint is experienced by the child or young person as an empowering one.

You may need to spend some time talking to the young person to allow them to feel confident that they have thought about the situation. Include them in the process as much as possible. This could include the young person writing down their complaint and working out what they would like to see as a resolution to it. Suggest they speak to the Children's Rights Officer or anyone else in a position to help and advise, who will support them with the complaint.

Complaints policy and procedure

Under the terms of Section 26(3) of the Children Act (1989), children, or the parents of those children placed with a fostering agency are entitled to make complaints and details of how these will be addressed will be contained in the Children's Services Guide. This will explain how a complaint can be made by or on behalf of children and will also give details of how to contact the Commission for Social Care Inspection.

There are usually two areas of complaints:

1. Those that are about the daily routine life in the foster home and may be moans, suggestions, disagreements and can be dealt with within the home.
2. Those that are serious and would need formal intervention.

Complaint type 2 would normally be those where there is a breach of a young person's health, safety or welfare and would normally be managed within the child protection procedures. The child protection procedures would take precedence over complaints investigations. The complaint investigation would include the outcomes of the child protection investigation within its findings and recommendations.

There are usually three levels to the complaints procedure:

- Level 1 – An informal approach to trying to resolve minor complaints.
- Level 2 – Where the complaint is investigated by the local authority/agency complaints officer.
- Level 3 – The introduction of an independent person to investigate and make recommendations about the complaint and its resolution.

Level 1 complaints are usually those issues that are not serious and can be resolved by listening to the young person and agreeing new terms e.g. bedtimes, airing disagreements or looking again at behaviour or sanctions used. Where at all possible, these should be addressed quickly, resolved and new agreements made with the child. If the issue persists, then the complaint will go to Level 2 or 3 and will be managed by an independent person. Check with the Children's Guide from your agency and the local authority for the details and time frames as well as what this entails. (See Chapter 29 Carers Making Complaints and Allegations Made Against Carers.)

Why do children and young people make complaints and allegations against carers?

These are some of the reasons:

- Carers or their family may have abused the child.
- Children may have a genuine grievance and have not been listened to.
- Young people you are likely to be caring for will have had extremely traumatic times even within their short lives and will probably have had their ability to trust, especially adults, distorted.
- They may be used to totally different boundaries and have been allowed to get on with their own thing and so resent the boundaries you have laid down.
- They may be seeking a way of taking control over their lives, be seeking attention or be desperate to get back to their parents.
- They may genuinely misinterpret an innocent action, such as a form of comfort (putting an arm around them) because this has had other significance in their lives.
- They are likely to repeat their learned patterns of behaviour and may be provocative, violent or abusive themselves.
- They may have learned that making unfounded threats or complaints has got them 'rewards' in the past.

However, do not lose sight of some of the obvious factors!

We can all remember those turbulent years, when we were teenagers, or in some case younger, when we were filled with doubts and uncertainties, as well as the excitement of entering the adult world. Young people will have all these. On top of this, they may be put into family situations when all they want is to rebel and to be their own person. But in placement, they will be expected to try to form attachments to you and your family – this is confusing and difficult at the best of times!

Chapter 29

Carers Making Complaints and Allegations Made Against Carers

Complaints and allegations

Information about the procedures to deal with investigations into allegations is made known to foster care staff, carers and children and young people and includes the provision of independent support to the foster carer(s) during an investigation.

NMS 22.9

NMS The National Minimum Standards also say the *fostering service* must ensure that:

- All fostering agencies must produce a Statement of Purpose which sets out the aims and objectives of their fostering service and has systems in place to ensure they meet the aims and objectives (**NMS 1**). The statement of purpose must include clear details about the right to complain about the fostering service (**NMS 1.4** and **22.8**).
- They keep records about complaints stored separately and securely (**NMS 25.2**) but are clearly recorded on the relevant files for staff, carers and children. This must include the conclusions and actions taken and the fostering agency must keep information that brings details of all complaints and allegations together so that these are reviewed and the necessary lessons learnt (**NMS 25.13**).
- All records and information about allegations of abuse are kept and monitored and there is a clear agency policy that states the circumstances in which a carer's name is to be removed from the foster care register (**NMS 22.10**).

UKNS The UK National Standards for Foster Care also include the following:

- That any person making a complaint or representation knows that they can call upon an independent support for any relevant meeting or discussion (**UKNS 25.6**).
- That those who have made a complaint receive a copy of the outcome within an agreed time limit set out in the agency's complaints procedure (**UKNS 25.7**).
- That each agency publishes an annual report on all the complaints and other issues that have been raised with them about the service they have provided, with details of the procedures they followed and the outcomes reached (**UKNS 25.9**).
- That the procedures for complaints and representations state that agencies must make specific arrangements for people whose first language is not English and those whose disability may make use of the procedures difficult (**UKNS 25.5**).

What does this mean for you?

It means that you have a right and a responsibility to make constructive complaints about the fostering service or any aspect of the service to the child.

You will need to have copies of the complaints procedure and this will give you details of what the procedure will do, by when and what type of outcomes you can expect.

Complaints procedures are usually devised around three levels:

- Level 1 – An informal approach to trying to resolve minor complaints.
- Level 2 – Where the complaint is investigated by the local authority/agency complaints officer.
- Level 3 – The introduction of an independent person to investigate and make recommendations about the complaint and its resolution.

Level 1 complaints are usually those issues that are not serious and can be resolved locally. You may have a complaint about any aspect of fostering. Where at all possible, these should be addressed quickly, resolved and new agreements forged. If the issue persists, then the complaint will go to Level 2 or 3 and will be managed by the agency complaints officer and then an independent person. Check the agency/local authority complaints procedures for the details and time frames as well as what this entails.

Allegations or complaints against carers

Allegations made against you will be one of the most distressing experiences as a carer. Research by the Fostering Network indicates that one in six carers will have a complaint or allegation made against them during their fostering career. However, there are many measures you can take to minimise the risk to yourselves and your family and many of them are contained in Chapter 19 *Safer Caring*.

Is there a difference between a complaint and an allegation?

For you it may feel that the two are exactly the same and may stir up the same range of emotions. For the sake of getting some clarity around what are highly emotional and potentially confusing processes, we will distinguish the differences below. However, *remember, safer caring and the existing procedures and guidance contained in this guide are there as much for your safety as for the young person's. It is always better to try to prevent something than to have to deal with it once it has occurred*.

An *allegation* against a carer is one where a child or young person is considered to be abused either emotionally, physically, sexually, or has been neglected by the carer. (For definitions of abuse see Chapter 20 *Child Protection*.) These allegations will be dealt with directly by the local authority where the child is living and they will use their child protection procedures. All the authorities who are involved with the child as well as your agency have a clear responsibility to assist in the investigations or with the on-going work that may transpire. The process, however, is clearly led and defined by the local authority.

A complaint against a carer is one where there are issues about the standard of care provided to the child/young person or there are differences of approaches to the needs of the young person. These would *not* normally be dealt with via child protection procedures although in some cases they may be. Child protection in these circumstances would be where the same complaint is made by the same young person at different times or other children have made similar complaints. Another situation may be if the complaint is considered to be emotionally abusive or is a result of negligence in your duty to keep the young person safe.

If the complaint were about the standard of care provided, for instance, issues about food, use of computer/internet, clothing, pocket money etc. then this would normally be dealt with by the young person's social worker and your supervising social worker. A meeting would be called in order to initially gain clarity about the situation and then seek practical remedies or agreements about behaviour. It would be expected that you and your supervising social worker, could agree:

- Coping mechanisms/strategies to prevent further complaints.
- That your agency will provide either individual or group training for you.
- That there will be a clear and written reaffirmation that you will abide by the terms of your foster carer agreement if a breach of this is acknowledged.
- If the allegation is serious or re-occurring, then your agency may consider suspending your approval/appointment and instigate termination of approval procedures.

Why do children/young people make complaints/allegations against carers? See Chapter 28 *Children Making Complaints*.

Chapter 30

Annual Reviews

Annual Reviews

A joint review is conducted with each carer at least once a year in a manner that satisfies the authority of the continuing capacity of the carer to carry out the fostering task, provides the carer with an opportunity to give feedback, contributes to essential information on the quality and range of service provided by the authority, and informs recruitment, assessment and training strategies.

UKNS 16

UKNS The UK National Standards also state that:

- The review be undertaken within an agreed format which not only assesses the way the foster carer(s) have performed but also encapsulates the carer's own assessment of the service and support they were given by the fostering service (**UKNS 16.1**).
- All statutory checks and references be updated within the required frequency (**UKNS 16.1 and 16.5**) – this is usually every three years but your agency may undertake this more frequently.
- The foster home should be inspected every year to ensure it can comfortably accommodate all who live there (**UKNS 6.1**).
- The report covering the review period is put together by your supervising social worker and includes reports from:
  - the social workers of the children you have looked after
  - all the children you have looked after
  - the children's parents
  - you
  - your children
  - any household members (**UKNS 16.2**).
- All review reports should contain action plans for up to the next 12 months that identify your training and support needs (**UKNS 16.3**).
- All review reports should also make clear the recommendation regarding your continued approval, the number of children and ages of children you are approved for and the category of care (**UKNS 16.3**).
- The carer should have the opportunity to see the report before it is presented to panel and make further comments should they wish to do so (**UKNS 16.4**).
- The reviews are chaired by somebody who knows about fostering but not directly involved, who can therefore draw independent conclusions and recommendations (**UKNS 16.6**).

→

- If a carer has a disability or needs translation or interpreting services, for instance, that this is provided to enable the carer to play as full a part in the review as is possible (**UKNS 16.7**).
- The review reports are presented to the fostering panel for their recommendation when there is:
  - a change in the carer's circumstances, household, availability etc
  - a recommendation to change the carer's approval category
  - a recommendation that the panel consider terminating approval.

  Then the panel must make a recommendation which will go to the agency decision-maker for the ultimate decision. The carer has a right to make representation to the panel which the panel will consider prior to making their recommendations (**UKNS 16.8**).
- The carer should receive written confirmation of the outcome of their review and this should contain details of their re-approval or not, changes in their terms of approval and the reasons for changes. Also, where appropriate, details of appeals or complaints procedure (**UKNS 16.9**).
- All the documentation obtained for the review should be recorded on the carer's file and this should include details of any comments, objections or complaints the carer may have made (**UKNS 16.10**).
- That a review can be undertaken in less than a year and if there has been a significant change, incident, complaint or allegation of abuse then this must be done so as soon as possible after the agency is notified (**UKNS 16.11**).

NMS The National Minimum Standards also say the *fostering service* must ensure that:

- The review report should include an appraisal of both the training needs and developmental needs of the carer for the following 12 months (**NMS 23.8**).

What does this mean for you?

Foster carers will be reviewed at least annually unless there is a reason to bring forward a review. The review should be undertaken by a person who knows about fostering but is not directly involved with your work.

An earlier review will be undertaken following a significant incident, complaint or allegation of abuse or neglect.

Why are annuals review carried out?

- It is a legal requirement.
- To gain re-approval for the following year. Where a termination of approval is being pursued by your agency, it gives a clear framework within which the necessary evidence and facts are gathered and comprehensively considered.

- It gives you the opportunity to go through the activities of your year and consider if your current approval category needs to be changed or to consider if you wish to continue to foster.
- It gives a focus for the views and wishes of your family, support network and any other relevant people who have been involved with you while you have been fostering to be considered.
- It gives you the opportunity to consider and plan for your needs for the following year. This is contained in the action plan to which you should have contributed.
- It gives you and your agency the opportunity to reflect on the training you have received and plan your training requirements for the following year.
- It should be used to reflect on knowledge and skills gained so you can measure your improvements and experiences of the previous year, along with the experiences of those of the rest of your family.
- It should consider the use of 'exemptions to the usual limit to foster' within your household i.e. – when the placements took you out of your approval category.

Who should contribute to an annual review?

- You – that includes your partner or spouse.
- The young person.
- The young person's social worker.
- Your supervising social worker.
- Your children.
- Members of your support network.
- The child's parent or guardian.
- Anyone else who can provide evidence about your period in fostering, e.g. teachers of the children you have cared for.

It is good practice to obtain information from your support network and any other source that could provide valuable evidence, however, as with this and the above list it is necessary to consider the appropriateness of pursuing some of these avenues. For instance, it may not always be possible to seek the views of the child or to approach a child's parent and there may be issues of confidentiality that would need to be carefully considered when approaching other agencies. These are factors that should be considered together with your supervising social worker when planning the review.

Your review should be conducted with all the fostering adults, an independent person and your supervising social worker and would usually be undertaken in your home. Your own children or children you foster may also be present for part of the time but this will usually depend upon how comfortable they are about it. They, along with others mentioned in the list above, should have been seen or specifically contacted for the review or been asked to make written contributions.

Your fostering agency should seek the views of social workers who have had children placed with you since the last review/since your approval but who may have already left your household. Where they can, they should also seek the views of the children.

When considering the review, the relevant extracts from the previous panel minutes must also be included and addressed forming part of the framework for the new review. This should be done by the supervising social worker as part of the report they prepare.

Once all the necessary forms have been completed, the evidence gathered and the review has been conducted, the next step is for it to go before the panel – see Chapter 7 *The Fostering Panel*.

What other things will be included in the annual review?

- The health and safety in your home and for the car. Your supervising social worker will go through this with you at least once a year. You will need to be familiar with the health and safety list and your supervising social worker will make recommendations with time frames for completion of any necessary tasks.
- A specific inspection of the child's room and equipment, toys, clothes etc that they have access to or belongs to them.
- Whether all the statutory checks are up-to-date – they should normally be reviewed at least every 3 years; or whether anyone else in your household needs to be checked.
- Whether the safer caring policy in your home incorporates the necessary changes to ensure the safety of all those involved in fostering with you. This includes guidance for your support network or guidelines about what to do when people visit your home.
- There should be one report of an unannounced visit undertaken to your home within the year.

What happens if we are told that my supervising social worker is going to recommend that our approval is not renewed? See Chapter 31 *Termination of Approval*.

Chapter 31

Termination of Approval

Termination of approval/agreement

Records about allegations of abuse are kept and monitored and there is a clear policy framework which outlines the circumstances in which a carer should be removed from the foster care register.

NMS 22.10

> **UKNS** The UK National Standards for Foster Care also include the following:
>
> - That when there is a recommendation to terminate the approval of a foster carer that the case is put before the fostering panel and the carer has a right to make their own representation and put their case before the panel (**UKNS 16.8**).

What does termination of approval mean?

The term 'termination of approval' simply means that you are not registered to foster and is a technical term so should not necessarily be interpreted as negative, as your approval may also be terminated just because you are no longer fostering. You may wish to leave the agency just by giving 28 days notice of your intention to resign. However, if your approval/foster care agreement *is* terminated by your agency then they would be obliged to make this known to anyone who seeks a reference about you. In extreme circumstances, your agency will have to notify the Commission for Social Care Inspection and it may affect any future police check you undertake. To recap, termination of approval is:

- When you have formally resigned from fostering or are just no longer fostering.
- Or when your approval to foster has been terminated by the agency decision maker. This would either be in recognition of the above two points or when you have been in breach of your foster care agreement.

Your agency can consider the termination of your approval/foster care agreement in the following circumstances (See Chapter 8 *The Foster Care Agreement*):

- Where the carers are in serious or continuing breach of its conditions as laid out in the foster care agreement. This includes any actual or perceived abuse of children, including your own and can also include continued low standards in child care.

- The carers consistently or regularly fails to meet the set requirements or the individual young person's care plan.
- The carer or anyone else living in the home is convicted in law as a Schedule 1 Offender or is charged or cautioned for an offence which would jeopardise the safety and stability of the placement and any further foster placements.

Even if your foster care agreement has been terminated, a report on you and the circumstances should still be placed before the panel which will consider your *approval* status. You will receive notification of the date of the panel and be given clear guidelines as to your right to appeal and the grounds these rights are recognised under. Even during this period you should still be supported by your agency and they may offer you the choice of being supported by someone outside the agency, e.g. someone from The Fostering Network. You will also still be covered by the insurance your agency will have provided for you.

If your agency intends to terminate your approval, this should not come as a surprise to you as you and your supervising social worker should have been discussing issues that would affect your continued approval.

Your supervising social worker would have had various meetings with you and will seek the same range of information as if conducting an annual review. You should be able to see the report and make comments and can also present your own evidence by attending the fostering panel.

If the panel recommends that you should no longer continue fostering and this is upheld by the decision-maker, then you will be notified in writing of the reasons and given 28 days to appeal against this decision to the agency decision-maker.

If you decide to appeal, the agency decision-maker will refer the matter back to the panel for further consideration. If the panel do not change their original recommendation, the decision-maker can either accept this or reject the recommendation. If the decision-maker feels there are sufficient grounds to terminate your approval then you will be notified of this as soon as possible in writing and this should include a full explanation.

What do I have to do if I want to leave my fostering agency or local authority?

Your agency should adhere to the Fostering Network/Independent Agencies Protocol for the movement of carers between agencies as detailed below. The protocol is based on the principal that, in all circumstances, the welfare of any children in placement must be the most important factor.

Fostering for most people may be work you choose to do for a relatively short period of time in your life, probably to fit into other things that are going on for you at that point. The fostering field is a fast developing one and carers have more choice over the agencies they may wish to work with. Terms and conditions and money are important factors. It is therefore recognised that you may wish to leave. If you do not have young people placed with you at the time and there are no outstanding issues, then it is just a matter of officially resigning. If there are outstanding matters, and in particular if you have a child placed with you, these matters will need to be planned, resolved or finalised. If you are involved in serious issues, such as a child protection investigation, inquiries will continue despite your resignation.

The Fostering Network/Independent Agencies Protocol

1. Each agency will include in their contract with carers a clause which makes it clear that no carer can join another agency (either local authority or independent fostering agency) whilst they have children in placement, unless arrangements for the continuing management of the placements are made to the satisfaction of both the placing authority and their fostering agency.

2. The contract will also make it clear that you must inform the existing agency in writing when you are considering such a move and that under no circumstances should an assessment by another agency begin before agreement is given.

3. When a carer has informed their current agency they wish to move, and when children are in placements, a meeting should take place between the agencies concerned and the child's local authority. This meeting should consider:
    - How these plans will affect the young person in place.
    - How the care plan should be maintained.
    - The on-going arrangements and responsibilities of your agency for this placement.
    - The protocol by which the new agency may use any future placements with you (foster carers).
    - The continuing arrangements for approving you as carers.
    - The views of the child, parent or any other interested party.
    If you wish to resign from your agency in order to join another agency but you still have a young person with you who is likely to remain for some significant time then you should also be mindful of the above.

4. The meeting must agree that the terms of the move are in the child's best interest and specify the particular arrangements that will govern the transfer and maintain the existing placements.

5. Where such arrangements are agreed to the satisfaction of the placing authority and your agency, the new agency may start the assessment and will request a proper reference from the placing authority and your agency. Your agency has a responsibility to provide such a reference when requested to do so.

6. Where such agreements cannot be reached, you must remain with your agency until any placement reaches its natural end. At this point you will be free to undertake the transfer.

7. Transfer will only be completed following a full re-assessment of you and your household by your new agency. This will include the new agency viewing your foster carer file.

Chapter 32

Whistle-blowing

Whistle-blowing

There is a whistle blowing policy which is made known to all staff and carers.

NMS 18.7

All of us, at one time or another will have concerns about something that may be happening at work or within our network. Usually these concerns are easily resolved. However, when they are of a serious nature, for instance, where you think children may be at risk, or where you think there may be something illegal or immoral going on, it can be difficult to know what to do.

You may be worried about raising these issues or want to keep them to yourself, as you may be scared, think it is none of your business or you have no proof. Or you may have told someone and they have not taken you seriously. Despite all these concerns, you would still be obliged, if you have a genuine suspicion and particularly if you have proof, to 'blow the whistle'. Your agency must have its own procedure which should make clear what your responsibilities are and how to use the whistle-blowing policy. This policy should also include how you will be protected from any unscrupulous backlash that may arise as well as give you a clear scope as to how far you are able to go in order to ensure that such bad practice is stopped.

The whistle-blowing policy should not be seen as an excuse to complain about a grievance you may have, in those circumstances, you should use the agency complaints procedure.

Appendix 1

The Foster Placement Agreement

Schedule 6, Regulation 34(3) The Fostering Services Regulations 2002

1. The Foster Placement Agreement is a document prepared by the *local authority that has responsibility for the child* or young person. It should contain all the information necessary to enable a foster carer to fully care for the child or young person. This information will be contained in the Looked After Children or Integrated Children's System documents but may also be a document provided specifically to fulfil the requirements of the Foster Placement Agreement.
   The information should include:
   - What the local authority's arrangements and plans are for the child and the aims and objectives of the placement.
   - Details of the child's history, religion, racial origin and cultural and linguistic background.
   - The child's health and identified health needs.
   - The safety needs of the child, including the need for special equipment or adaptions.
   - The child's educational needs.
   - Any needs the child may have arising from any disability or special need.

2. The local authority's arrangements for financially supporting the child during the placement.

3. The local authority's arrangements for giving consent to medical or dental treatment.

4. The local authority's arrangements for giving consent to a child taking part in school trips or staying overnight away from the foster parent's home.

5. Details of all visits to the child by social workers or other authorised people, with details of frequency and reviews.

6. Details of all contact arrangements to the child from parents or any other interested parties and details of court orders relating to contact.

7. Confirmation from the foster carer as to their compliance to the foster care agreement (see Chapter 8 *The Foster Care Agreement*).

8. Confirmation from the foster carer of their co-operation with the local authority regarding the arrangements for the child.

NB: the use of the term local authority on this page refers to the local authority with responsibility for the child.

Appendix 2

The Foster Care Register

Schedule 2, Regulation 22 The Fostering Services Regulations 2002

1. Schedule 2 states that a register should be kept of each child placed with foster carers and the register should contain the following information:
   - The date of the placement.
   - The name and address of the foster carer.
   - The date the placement ended.
   - The child's address prior to the placement.
   - The child's address on leaving the placement.
   - The child's local authority.
   - The regulations under which the child was placed with the foster carers.

2. Schedule 2 also requires a record that details each person working for the fostering service provider including:
   - Full name.
   - Gender.
   - Date of birth.
   - Home address.
   - Details of child care qualifications and experience of working with children.
   - Details of employment contract and status.
   - Number of hours worked and whether employed on a full-time or part-time basis.

3. A record of all accidents occurring to children whilst placed with foster parents.

If you stop fostering or your approval to foster is terminated, your fostering agency will remove your name from the Foster Care Register.

Appendix 3

The Statement of Purpose

Standard 1 National Minimum Standards

- The statement of purpose is a document required by all fostering services providers that sets out its aims and objectives and ensures that they meet those aims and objectives.
- The statement of purpose clearly lists the services provided for children who are placed by the fostering service. If additional services, for instance, education, health or therapeutic services are provided, then these should be covered in the statement of purpose.
- The registered provider* (in the case of a local authority, the elected members) formally approve the statement of purpose, review, update and modify it at least annually.
- The statement of purpose includes details of the following:
  - Its status and constitution (agencies only).
  - Its management structure.
  - The services it provides.
  - Its aims and objectives, principles and standards of care.
  - Numbers of staff, their qualifications and experiences.
  - Numbers of foster carers.
  - Numbers of children placed.
  - Numbers of complaints and their outcomes.
  - The procedure and processes for recruiting, approving, training, supporting and reviewing carers.
- The statement of purpose states that the fostering service provides a Children's Guide suitable for all the children fostered and which includes a summary of what the service sets out to do for children. This guide is to be given to all children fostered by the service as soon as they are placed. A copy is also to be given to all foster carers. The statement of purpose also requires, where necessary, for the guide to be produced in different formats to meet the differing needs of children looked after by that service. The guide should contain specific information on how the child can gain access to an independent advocate and about how to complain.
- The statement of purpose requires that all policies, procedures and written guidance to staff and carers accurately reflect the statement of purpose.

* Registered provider is the person registered with the National Care Standards Commission/ Commission for Social Care Inspection who provides the fostering service for the agency.

Appendix 4

Useful Contact Details for Children Looked After

A National Voice (ANV), Central Hall, Oldham Street, Manchester M1 1JT. Tel: 0161 237 5577. They also have a website: www.anationalvoice.org

British Agencies for Adoption and Fostering (BAAF), Skyline House, 200 Union Street, London SE1 0LY. Tel: 020 7278 2000. They also have a website: www.baaf.org.uk

Children's Legal Centre. Tel: 01206 872466. Free legal advice or information on all aspects of the law as it affects children and young people. Children's Rights Officers and Advocates. Tel 020 7833 2100.

Fostering Network, 87 Blackfriars Road, London SE1 8HA. Help line Tel: 0207 620 2100. They also have a website: www.fostering.net

Kidscape, 2 Grosvenor Gardens, London SW1W 0HD. Tel: 020 7730 3300. They also have a website: www.kidscape.org.uk

National Care Standards Commission (NCSC), Children's Rights Director (Roger Morgan), St. Nicholas Building, St. Nicholas Street, Newcastle upon Tyne, NE1 1NB. Tel: 0191 233 3600.

National Youth Advocacy Service (NYAS), 99-105 Argyle Street, Birkenhead, Wirral CN41 6AD. Freephone: 0800 616101. They also have a website: www.nyas.net.uk

The Voice for the Child in Care, Unit 4, Pride Court, 80-82 White Lion Street, London N1 9PF. Tel: 0207 833 5792. – this line will also get young people straight to an advisor or young people can use Freephone: 0808 800 5792. They also have a website: www.vcc-uk.org

WHO CARES Trust. Young people can write to the trust for advice and information or ring Who Cares Linkline: Freephone 0800 800 500. The Trust publishes a magazine for young people in care. They also have a website: www.thewhocarestrust.org

Bibliography

BAAF (2000) BAAF Form F. BAAF.

Chambers, H. (2003) *Draft National Healthy Care Standard (NHCS) Proposals for National Roll out Within the Children's Policy Agenda: Evaluation Report.* National Children's Bureau.

Department of Education and Skills (2004) Integrated Children's System website, Integrated Children's System – Exemplars – Documents, Crown Copyright 1995-2004.

Department of Education and Skills, Integrated Children's System website, Integrated Children's System, Briefing Paper No 5, HMSO.

Department of Health (2000) *Children (Leaving Care) Act 2000*.

Department of Health (2002) *Fostering Regulations 2002*. HMSO.

Department of Health (2002) *Education Protects: Summary for Foster Carers*. Crown copyright.

Department of Health (2002) *National Minimum Standards for Fostering Services*. HMSO.

Fostering Network (2000) *Guide to Competency Assessment and Materials*. NFCA.

Fostering Network (2002) *Safer Caring*. NFCA.

Fostering Network (1990) *Training Materials on Managing Behaviour: A Problem Shared*. Fostering Network.

Hayes, D. and Callaghan, D. (2003) 'Government Cuts Education Targets in Wake of Poor Examination Results'. *Community Care*. 24-30 April.

Kidscape (2001) *Keep Them Safe*. www.kidscape.org.uk

Lord, J., Barker, S. and Cullen, D. (2000) *Effective Panels*. BAAF.

Olle, H. (2003) *National Healthy Care Standard Pilot Project: Evaluation Report*. National Children's Bureau.

UK Joint Working Party on Foster Care (1999) *Code of Practice on the Recruitment, Assessment, Approval, Training, Management and Support of Foster Carers*. NFCA.

UK Joint Working Party on Foster Care (1999) *Report and Recommendations of the UK Joint Working Party on Foster Care*. NFCA.

UK Joint Working Party on Foster Care (1999) *UK National Standards for Foster Care*. NFCA.

United Nations (1989) *The Convention on the Rights of the Child*. UNICEF

Valios, N. (2003) 'Final Frontier?' *Community Care*. 7-11 August.

Wheal, A. in consultation with NFCA, BAAF and CETSW (1995) *The Foster Carer's Handbook*. Russell House Publishing.